TACTICS

STUDY GUIDE

UPDATED AND EXPANDED

A GUIDE TO EFFECTIVELY DISCUSSING
YOUR CHRISTIAN CONVICTIONS

GREGORY KOUKL

ZONDERVAN REFLECTIVE

Tactics Study Guide plus Streaming Video, Updated and Expanded

Published in Grand Rapids, Michigan, by Zondervan. Zondervan is a registered trademark of The Zondervan Corporation, L.L.C., a wholly owned subsidiary of HarperCollins Christian Publishing, Inc.

Requests for information should be addressed to customercare@harpercollins.com.

Zondervan titles may be purchased in bulk for educational, business, fundraising, or sales promotional use. For information, please email SpecialMarkets@Zondervan.com.

ISBN 978-0-310-17963-4 (softcover)
ISBN 978-0-310-11974-6 (ebook)

Published in association with the literary agency of Mark Sweeney & Associates, Bonita Springs, Florida 34135.

Cover photo: iStockphoto.com

Printed in the United States of America

25 26 27 28 29 30 31 32 33 34 35 36 37 38 39 40 /TRM/ 15 14 13 12 11 10 9 8 7 6 5 4 3 2 1

Contents

STUDY GUIDE INSTRUCTIONS

An Adventure in Learning

You are about to embark on an exciting adventure in learning with one of the finest training tools available. *Tactics Study Guide: A Guide to Effectively Discussing Your Christian Convictions,* together with the accompanying *Tactics Video Study,* provides an easy-to-follow, well-reasoned plan for mastering the art of maneuvering in conversations about spiritual things.

Though the information may be a little challenging at first, by faithfully going through this material you will not only learn it for yourself, but should by the end be able to teach someone else.

In eight one-hour sessions, you will learn how to do the following:

- Initiate conversations effortlessly
- Stop challengers in their tracks and turn the tables
- Graciously and effectively expose faulty thinking
- Maneuver through minefields
- Present the truth clearly, cleverly, and persuasively

USING THIS STUDY GUIDE

The *Tactics Study Guide* is meant to be easy to use. It's designed so you can readily see the relationships between the main ideas. You'll also notice that the text is punctuated by special sections, each with its own unique purpose.

AMBASSADOR SKILLS

These sidebars give tips that will help you improve your tactical skills when using your new knowledge so you can present the arguments in a winsome and attractive way.

INTERACTIVE STUDY

These important segments are designed to take your training experience from the passive stage to the active stage. If you're going through this study on your own, you will sometimes need to enlist the help of another person or even a few people for these sections. Exercises include discussion, role-playing, recall, directed reflection, and memory tips.

REFLECT FOR A MOMENT

These segments give you a chance to momentarily step aside from the main point and ponder a related idea. It may be an insight, a clever application, or a reflection designed to make the lesson more practical or meaningful.

GOING DEEPER: Information for Self-Study

Here you will find additional information to study on your own that is not included either in this study guide or the accompanying video study.

SELF-ASSESSMENT

A critical element of mastery learning is recall, the ability to bring to mind the important details you've been learning. These self-assessment quizzes are a powerful tool to help fix the salient details of the course in your mind so you can recall them quickly when you need them in the future.

DEMONSTRATING MASTERY

At the beginning of each new session, you will find a review of the "Self-Assessment" material from the preceding session. Be sure to do this exercise—either on your own or with someone else—before each session. It has two purposes. First, by working to recall the main points of the prior session, the ideas will be reinforced in your mind. Second, by reviewing the past material, you will be prepped for the next session.

FOOD FOR THOUGHT

Additional articles are included at the end of each session to supplement your learning experience. They expand on concepts or principles dealt with during the sessions.

NOTES

The final section of each session has notes that either document the information taught in the manual or offer added insight. You may want to use the references as a guide to additional resources for further study.

THE SECRET TO MASTERY LEARNING

Finally, here is one secret that guarantees mastery of this material: Teach it to others. Anyone who is a student of the material can become a teacher of the material. Perhaps you can give talks in your church, Sunday school, youth group, homeschool, or small group using the notes in your manual and adapting the material to your unique situation.

Whatever way you choose to pass the material on, the benefit will be twofold: You'll gain a better mastery of the material by teaching it, and whoever you share it with will benefit as well.

SESSION 1

Getting You into the Driver's Seat: Learning the Columbo Tactic

I. INTRODUCTION

A. This course could change everything for you.

1. You may look back on the time you spent learning this material and mark it as a turning point in your life in the way you engage other people for the Gospel.
2. I say this with some confidence because this is exactly what countless numbers of people have told me over the years. Tactics changed everything for them.

B. The tactical approach you will learn in this course will give you two indispensable skills to help you engage others about your Christian convictions.

1. First, it will train you to maneuver comfortably and graciously in conversations with those who disagree with you.
2. Second, it will teach you the art of maintaining appropriate control—what I call "staying in the driver's seat"—in your discussions with others.

INTERACTIVE STUDY

Pair up with another person and explain your answer to the following question: When I think about discussing Christianity with nonbelievers . . .

- I relish the encounter.
- I'm willing, but nervous and uncertain.
- It scares me, but I try anyway.
- I try to avoid it.

C. The missing piece

1. Going to conferences and pursuing individual study provides lots of information, but there's something missing.
2. There's a missing bridge that helps you get from the content to the conversation, from the scholarship to the relationship.
3. In this course I want to give you that missing bridge.

D. Goals for the first session

1. First, I'll define tactics and warn you of some dangers of using a tactical approach.
2. Second, I'll suggest a significant change in the way you approach evangelism.
3. Third, I'll introduce you to the first and most powerful tactic, the one that is the core of our game plan.

GOING DEEPER: Information for Self-Study

Apologetics has a questionable reputation with some Christians. By definition, apologists "defend" the faith. They "defeat" false ideas. They "destroy" speculations raised up against the knowledge of God. Those sound like fightin' words to many people. It's not surprising, then, that believers and unbelievers alike associate apologetics with conflict. In their view, defenders don't dialogue; they fight.

In addition to the image problem, apologists face another barrier. The truth is that effective apologetics nowadays requires more than having the right answers. It's too easy for some people to ignore our facts, deny our claims, or simply yawn and walk away.

Then again, sometimes they don't walk away. They stand and fight. They wade into battle and fire a barrage we can't handle. Caught off balance, we tuck our tails between our legs and retreat, maybe for good.

I'd like to suggest a "more excellent way." Jesus said that when you find yourself a sheep amid wolves, be innocent but shrewd (Matt. 10:16). This calls for a tactical approach. Even though real spiritual warfare is going on,[1] our engagements should look more like diplomacy than D-Day.

II. OUR NEED FOR TACTICS, WHAT THEY ARE, AND HOW TO USE THEM

A. Our need for tactics concerns our commission to be effective ambassadors for Christ (2 Cor. 5:20).

1. Ambassadors have three essential skills.
    a. Knowledge: an accurately informed mind
    b. Wisdom: an artful method
    c. Character: an attractive manner
2. These skills play a part in every effective engagement we have with a nonbeliever.
3. The second skill—the artful method, or "tactical wisdom"—is the focus of this course.

B. Tactics are distinct from strategy.

1. Strategy involves the big picture, the large-scale operation, one's positioning prior to engagement.
    a. I use the term *strategy* in reference to the tremendous resources of knowledge available to us to be adequately prepared to give an account for the hope that is in us (1 Peter 3:15).
        1) In our case, Christianity has strategic superiority—it is well "positioned" on the battlefield—because our ideas can hold up under serious scrutiny compared to other views.

2) We have an excellent case. We have the best answers to life's most important questions.

b. Our strategy concerns the content, information, and reasons why someone should believe that Christianity describes the world accurately, all of which fall under the heading of either defensive or offensive apologetics.[2]

1) Defensive apologetics answers direct challenges to Christianity. For example . . .

(a) It responds to attacks on the Bible's authority.

(b) It answers the problem of evil.

(c) It addresses Darwinian macroevolution.

2) Offensive apologetics makes a positive case for Christianity. For example . . .

(a) It provides evidence for the existence of God.

(b) It supplies evidence for the resurrection of Christ.

(c) It presents evidence of fulfilled prophecy.

c. Our strategic concerns include a number of contemporary issues.

1) The radical relativism and skepticism of postmodernism that denies the existence of objective truth.[3] This would include moral relativism (all moral truth is individual or group based) and religious pluralism (all religions are equally valid and "true" for those who believe).

2) The competing views on Jesus' identity.

3) The problem of evil.

4) The ethical issues of abortion, homosexuality, human cloning, doctor-assisted suicide, and the nature of marriage.

5) The historical accuracy of the Gospels.

2. In contrast, tactics literally refer to "the art of arranging," deploying one's assets, the details of the engagement.

a. Tactics, simply put, are about how we maneuver in conversations, allowing us to:

1) Use our knowledge in creative ways.
2) Choreograph the particulars of our response.
3) Style our response to objections.
4) Employ specific methods in addressing attacks.
5) Guide us with sound reasoning, clear thinking, and aggressive advocacy.

b. Often a clever commander has the advantage over a superior opponent through deft tactical maneuvering.

c. Tactics are not:

1) Tricks or slick ruses.
2) Clever ploys to destroy non-Christians, forcing them to submit to your point of view.
3) Attempts to belittle or humiliate or add notches in your spiritual belt.

d. Instead, tactics help you:

1) Manage, not manipulate.
2) Control, not coerce.
3) Finesse, not fight.
4) Navigate through the minefields.
5) Put you in the driver's seat of the conversation.

e. I offer these warnings about tactics for two reasons.

1) First, tactics are powerful and can be easily abused. It's not difficult to make someone look silly with these techniques.
2) Second, because the illustrations in this workbook are abbreviated accounts, they may appear harsher, more direct, or more aggressive on the page than they were in reality.

f. I do mean to be direct, focused, and challenging.

g. I do not mean to be abrasive, abusive, or alarming.

h. The goal is to find clever ways to exploit another's bad thinking for the purpose of guiding him or her to truth, yet remaining gracious and charitable at the same time.

REFLECT FOR A MOMENT

"It is not the Christian life to wound, embarrass, or play one-upmanship with colleagues, friends, or even opponents, but it's a common vice that anyone can easily fall into."[4]

—Hugh Hewitt

III. GARDENING VS. HARVESTING

A. Key insight: Before there can be any harvest, there must always be a season of gardening.

1. This insight has completely changed my approach to my conversations with non-Christians. Virtually no one becomes a Christian overnight, especially nowadays.
2. Jesus said:

   Don't you have a saying, "It's still four months until harvest"? I tell you, open your eyes and look at the fields! They are ripe for harvest. Even now the one who reaps draws a wage and harvests a crop for eternal life, so that the sower and the reaper may be glad together. Thus the saying "One sows and another reaps" is true. I sent you to reap what you have not worked for. Others have done the hard work, and you have reaped the benefits of their labor. (John 4:35–38 NIV)

B. Notice the breakdown:

1. Two seasons: gardening and harvesting
2. Two kinds of workers: sowers and reapers
3. One team, with everyone rejoicing together!

C. What kind of worker are you, a gardener or a harvester?

1. Gardening takes more work than harvesting, since harvesting is easy when the fruit is ripe.
2. So we probably need more gardeners than harvesters.
3. I'm a gardener, and I bet you are too, at least most of the time you talk with others about spiritual things.
4. And maybe you've been sitting on the bench out of play because you weren't a harvester. Now you know where you can make a difference: gardening.

D. My modified goal:

1. Since I'm a gardener, I'm not focused on harvesting.
2. My main goal is simply to "put a stone in their shoe."
   a. I want to annoy them in a good way.
   b. I want to get them thinking.
   c. I want them to see that Jesus is worth thinking about.

IV. THE TACTICAL GAME PLAN

A. Here is my promise to you:

1. I am going to give you a game plan that will allow you to converse with confidence in any situation.
2. It does not matter how little you know, or how knowledgeable or aggressive or obnoxious the other person may be.

B. It's a game plan that's simple to follow, yet is tailor-made for each individual and will help keep you in the driver's seat in conversations.

1. Note these instructions by the Apostle Paul:

> Conduct yourselves with wisdom toward outsiders, making the most of the opportunity. Let your speech always be with grace, as though seasoned with salt, so that you will know how you should respond to each person. (Col. 4:5–6 NASB)

2. In other words, be smart, be nice, and be tactical.

C. When I talk about "staying in the driver's seat," I mean being in control in your interactions with nonbelievers.

For instance, notice how I was able to use the tactical approach to maneuver smoothly in a conversation with a young woman at a photo center.

GREG: [This conversation began when I noticed a pentagram—a five-pointed star—she wore around her neck.] Does that necklace have religious significance, or is it just jewelry?

WOMAN: Yes, it has religious significance. The five points stand for earth, wind, fire, water, and spirit.

GREG: Does it have religious significance for *you*, personally?

WOMAN: Yes. I'm a pagan. It's an earth religion.

GREG: So, you're Wiccan? [a student of witchcraft]

WOMAN: Yes. We respect all life.

GREG: So, then, that would make you pro-life regarding abortion, right?

WOMAN: No. I'm pro-choice.

GREG: That surprises me. Isn't it unusual for someone in Wicca to be pro-choice?

WOMAN: Well, I know I could never do that. I could never kill a baby. [Note her choice of words—"kill a baby."] I wouldn't do anything to hurt anyone else, because it might come back on me, kind of like karma.

GREG: But shouldn't we do something to stop *other* people from killing babies?

WOMAN: I think women should have a choice.

GREG: Women should have the choice to kill their own babies? [Note my use of her original words here.]

WOMAN: Well . . . I think all things should be taken into consideration on this question.

GREG: Okay, tell me what kind of considerations would make it okay to kill a baby?

WOMAN: [*quickly*] Incest.

GREG: Let me see if I understand you correctly. If I had a two-year-old child here next to me who had been conceived through incest, in your view I could kill her. Is that right?

WOMAN: [*pausing*] Well, I guess I'd have mixed feelings about that.

AMBASSADOR SKILLS

When discussing controversial issues, be careful not to resort to slick rhetoric—empty slogans, loaded words, ridicule, or name-calling. This is misleading and unkind, and it won't persuade a critic. Use a reasonable argument instead.[5]

1. In this short encounter, I used three foundational tactics to help me challenge the young woman's faulty thinking.
   a. First, I asked nine questions.
      1) I used these questions to begin the conversation and gather information from her.
      2) I also used these questions to exploit weaknesses in what she said.
   b. I tried to show the inconsistent and contradictory nature of her views.
      1) On the one hand, she is a witch who respects all life.
      2) On the other hand, she is pro-choice on abortion, a procedure she characterized as "killing babies."
   c. Third, I used a tactic that allowed me to show her the logical consequences of her beliefs.
      1) She thought incest was a legitimate reason to "kill a baby."
      2) I asked her about a toddler who was conceived through incest.

3) We were left, through her reasoning, with a legitimate reason to kill this toddler.

2. The value of using the tactical approach is, simply put, to help you stay in the driver's seat of the conversation.
   a. It allows you to productively direct the discussion.
   b. It forces the other person to do most of the work.
   c. It helps avoid conflict. Remember, if anyone gets mad, you're going to lose your chance at making a difference.

D. Regardless of your present skill level, you can learn to maneuver almost effortlessly in conversations if you commit to learning the material in this study.

1. This study has equipped thousands of people like you with the confidence and ability to have meaningful, productive conversations about spiritual things.
2. This study guide covers almost everything presented in the accompanying videos, relieving you of the need to take extensive notes.

AMBASSADOR SKILLS

Tactics require you to think actively and give mental attention to what's going on. The approach resembles one-on-one basketball more than chess, involving constant motion, adjustment, and adaptation. The tactical approach requires as much careful listening as it does thoughtful response.

GOING DEEPER: Information for Self-Study

Let me offer you a word of encouragement. I've been defending the faith actively and "professionally" for more than three decades in the marketplace of ideas with people who oppose evangelical Christian views and are professionals in their own right—atheists, skeptics, Mormons, Jewish rabbis, and secularists of all sorts.

When I started, I wasn't sure how I would fare in public against the pros with thousands of people listening on radio or TV. I discovered that the facts and sound reason are on our side. We don't have to be frightened of the truth or the opposition if we do our homework. After all, even people who don't like tests don't mind them much when they know the answers.

The truth is this: The Gospel can be defended if it is properly understood and properly articulated. If we take our time and think through the issues, we can make a solid defense. If we have the truth, the opposing argument will always have a flaw. Keep looking for it. Sooner or later it will show up. The right tactic can help you discover the flaw in another person's thinking and show it for the error it is.

Remember this: Intelligent people still make foolish mistakes in thinking when it comes to spiritual things. The tactics you learn in this class will help you exploit those mistakes. You'll discover that people don't give much thought to their objections. How do I know? Because I listen to the objections.

INTERACTIVE STUDY

Ten-Second Window

Pair up with another person and consider the following real-world scenarios. In each scenario, you have a ten-second window of time to create an opportunity for further dialogue with the other individual. What would you do or say in each situation?

Scenario 1: "There Is No God"

The Scene: You're at a dinner party at your friend's home with some of your close friends from church. The conversation ranges naturally over a number of interesting spiritual topics. Suddenly, to your surprise and embarrassment, the host's fifteen-year-old son announces with some belligerence that he doesn't believe in God anymore. "It's simply not rational," he says. "There is no proof." No one had any idea he'd been moving in this direction. There's a stunned silence.

The Challenge: Your opportunity will pass quickly. You have only a few seconds to initiate further dialogue, but you want to do so in a way that is productive and will help everyone in the room to reflect intelligently on the issue. What will you say?

Scenario 2: Religious Pluralism

The Scene: It's the night of your weekly Bible study group. During the discussion of the Sunday sermon on the Great Commission, a newcomer remarks, "Who are we to say Christianity is better than any other religion? I think the essence of Jesus' teaching is love, the same as all religions, not telling other people how to live or believe." The rest of the group fidgets awkwardly, but says nothing.

The Challenge: You're concerned about your friend's statement and want to say something, but you're also concerned about not sounding narrow-minded or intolerant. No one else is speaking up, and you have only a few seconds before you lose the opportunity to represent God's view on other religions. What will you say?

Scenario 3: The Bible

The Scene: You're riding the university shuttle with a friend who notices a Bible in your backpack. "I've read the Bible before," he says. "It's got some interesting stories, but people take it too seriously. It was only written by men, after all, and men make mistakes." You try to recall the points your pastor made a few weeks before about the Bible's inspiration, but come up empty-handed.

The Challenge: You didn't know your friend had any exposure to the Bible until now. You're concerned about keeping the conversation productive while being sensitive to the fact that other shuttle riders are listening. What do you say in response?

V. LEARNING THE COLUMBO TACTIC

A. The Columbo tactic is the "Queen Mother" of all tactics.

1. It's easily combined with the other tactics.

2. It's the simplest tactic imaginable to stop a challenger in his tracks, turn the tables, and get him thinking.
3. Plus, it's an almost effortless way to put you in the driver's seat of the conversation.

REFLECT FOR A MOMENT

It's not unusual for a Christian to get tongue-tied, not knowing what to say for fear of offending someone. The Columbo tactic provides a step-by-step game plan to help you ease into the process, making it easy even for the most timid to engage others in a meaningful and productive way.

B. The Columbo tactic is named for Lieutenant Columbo of the long-running television series *Columbo*, a brilliant detective who appears bumbling, inept, and completely harmless.
   1. With his rumpled trench coat, stub of a cigar, and borrowed pencil, Columbo looks like he couldn't think his way out of a wet paper bag.
   2. While putting his foes at ease with his harmless demeanor, Columbo then employs his trademark approach:
      a. "I got a problem. Something about this thing bothers me. Maybe you can clear this up for me. *Do you mind if I ask you a question?*"
      b. "Thank you. You're a very intelligent person. Oh, just one more thing."
      c. "I'm sorry. I'm making a pest of myself. It's because I keep asking these questions. But I can't help it. It's a habit."
   3. This is a habit you want to get into!

C. The key to the Columbo tactic: Go on the offensive in an inoffensive way with carefully selected questions that productively advance the conversation.
   1. Simply put, if you hit a roadblock, ask a question.
      a. Never make an assertion when a question can make the same point.

b. With planning and practice, this tactic can become second nature.

2. Using questions offers tremendous advantages.
   a. Questions are interactive, inviting others to participate.
   b. Questions make headway without requiring you to state your case.
   c. Questions shift the burden of proof to the other person.
   d. Most importantly, the Columbo tactic puts you in the driver's seat.
3. The technique is particularly useful where you work. It makes it possible for you to subtly move your case forward without "preaching" at others.

REFLECT FOR A MOMENT

Once, while at the home of a well-known actor, I got into a long conversation with the actor's wife about animal rights. I had serious reservations about her ideas, but I didn't contradict her directly. Instead, I kept asking questions meant to expose some of the weaknesses I saw in her view.

Eventually she went on the offensive and began to challenge what she thought were my views. I then pointed out I had never actually stated my beliefs. I had simply asked questions. Since I had never asserted my own view then, strictly speaking, I had nothing to defend.

Once we make a claim in a discussion, others have every right to ask us for evidence. Until then, though, we're off the hook.

INTERACTIVE STUDY

In the space below, sum up the Columbo tactic in one sentence.

D. The Columbo tactic is your game plan. It has three unique applications,[6] each launched with a different kind of question.[7]

1. The tactical game plan provides you with an easy-to-apply, step-by-step approach to having conversations about your convictions.
2. It gives you an incredible margin of safety, since asking questions instead of making statements or claims protects you from having to defend a view.
3. The plan makes it easy to pursue friendly conversation and avoid unnecessary conflict.

REFLECT FOR A MOMENT

"Ask at least a half dozen questions in every conversation."[8]

—Hugh Hewitt

This skill at inquiry will immediately mark you as different and attractive . . . When you ask a question, you are displaying interest in the person asked—and in most settings this is a great boon to the pride and self-worth of the person being asked. Most people are not queried on many, if any, subjects. Their opinions are not solicited. To ask them is to be remembered fondly as a very interesting and gracious person in your own right.

Once developed, the habit of asking questions will inevitably give you advantages in every setting. You will obviously leave most situations with more information (and friends) than when you arrived, and being an asker allows you control of situations that statement makers rarely achieve. Once you learn how to guide a conversation, you have also learned how to control it. You can express your own opinions as questions, and every human emotion can be conveyed this way.

An alert questioner can judge when someone grows uneasy. But don't stop. Just change directions.[9]

E. The first application of the Columbo tactic is to gather information.

1. The very first thing you want to do in any conversation—before you do anything else—is to use questions to get the lay of the land. Think of it as gathering "intel." You almost always need more information to know how to proceed further.
2. This is the simplest way to use the Columbo tactic. It is virtually effortless, putting no pressure on you at all.
3. When used this way, a question can:
   a. Be a casual conversation-starter (like with the witch in Wisconsin).
   b. Buy you valuable time.
   c. Alert you to weaknesses, flaws, or ambiguities.
   d. Give you valuable information for this and future encounters.
4. Use this Columbo question: "What do you mean by that?" (or some variation).
   a. This is a clarification question that helps you learn *what* a person thinks so you don't misunderstand her or, worse, misrepresent her.
   b. This question should be delivered in a mild, genuinely inquisitive fashion.
   c. It also forces the person to be precise in her meaning, as many people object to Christianity for reasons they haven't completely thought through themselves.

AMBASSADOR SKILLS

Misrepresenting a view, even by accident, is a serious misstep. When we distort someone's view—especially when we make it appear weaker than it is—we are committing the straw-man fallacy—setting up a lifeless imitation of a friend's view (the "straw man") that we easily knock down, instead of dealing with his actual view. If you're guilty of setting up a straw man, you may find you've given a brilliant refutation of a view that the other person does not hold.

5. Here are some examples of the Columbo tactic in action.
   a. When someone says, "There is no God," ask them, "What do you mean by 'God'?" If they mean an old man with a beard who sits on a throne out in space, Christians don't believe in that kind of God, either. Maybe they reject the God of organized religion, but still believe in some divine "force." Maybe they don't believe in anything outside the natural realm. It's pointless to talk further unless you have a clear idea of what they mean.
   b. When someone says, "All religions are basically the same," ask, "Really? In what way are they basically the same?" The point here is not to determine if there are similarities between religions (there often are), but whether the similarities are weightier than the differences. After all, God cannot be both a personal being (Judaism, Christianity, and Islam) and a non-personal being (forms of Hinduism) at the same time.
   c. When someone says, "You shouldn't force your views on me," ask, "Specifically, how am I *forcing* my views on you?"
   d. When someone says, "That's just your interpretation," ask, "What do you mean by 'just'?" Although you are giving your interpretation (your understanding of the true meaning of the text), you need to find out if he believes all interpretations are equally valid and yours is "just" one of them. Where does he think your "interpretation" has gone wrong?
   e. When someone says, "Miracle stories were added to the Bible," ask, "What do you mean by 'added to'?" Here you're trying to determine how someone adds lines of text to thousands of handwritten documents circulating around the Mediterranean region in the first few centuries. This problem applies to any claim that the Bible has been purposefully altered.
   f. When someone says, "The Bible has been changed through copying and recopying over the years," ask, "How do you think it has been altered?" You need to find out if he's familiar with the study of the written transmission of ancient texts (called "textual criticism") or is he just repeating something he's heard.

g. When someone says, "How could God exist when there is so much evil in the world?" ask, "What do you mean by 'evil'?" or "What, in your mind, is the conflict?" As it turns out, evil doesn't provide good evidence *against* God, but *for* God, since God must exist to provide the objective standard of good by which any evil is measured.[10]

Important: In each case, have the person *spell out* the objection.

6. This first Columbo question accomplishes five important objectives:
   a. First, it immediately engages your friend in an interactive way.
   b. Second, it flatters him because it shows genuine interest in his view.
   c. Third, it forces him to think more carefully and more precisely—maybe for the first time—about his intended meaning.
   d. Fourth, it gives you valuable information about your friend's exact position.
   e. Fifth, it puts you in the driver's seat of the conversation.
7. Be sure to pay attention to the response.
   a. If it is unclear, follow up with more clarification questions.
   b. Say, "Let me see if I understand you on this . . . ," then feed back the view to make sure you got it right.
8. By the way, don't be surprised if you get the "sounds of silence" response when you ask this question.
   a. Some people merely repeat what they've been socialized to say and have never really thought about what they actually mean.
   b. When asked for clarification, they get caught flat-footed and don't know how to respond.
   c. Your questions graciously prod them to actually think through their view, maybe for the first time. So wait them out and give them time to think before jumping in again.

Do not underestimate the power of the question "What do you mean by that?" (or some variation). Use it often. You can ask this question all day long with absolutely no pressure on you.

INTERACTIVE STUDY

Ten-Second Window Redux

The Ten-Second Window scenarios are printed below. Pair up with a partner and role-play these scenarios using the first Columbo question. Develop a quick response to each scenario using some variation of the question "What do you mean by that?" Remember to choose a question that applies specifically to the particular issue at hand.

Scenario 1: "There Is No God"

The Scene: You're at a dinner party at your friend's home with some of your close friends from church. The conversation ranges naturally over a number of interesting spiritual topics. Suddenly, to your surprise and embarrassment, the host's fifteen-year-old son announces with some belligerence that he doesn't believe in God any more. "It's simply not rational," he says. "There is no proof." No one had any idea he'd been moving in this direction. There's a stunned silence. What will you say?

Columbo Questions:

____

____

____

Scenario 2: Religious Pluralism

The Scene: It's the night of your weekly Bible study group. During the discussion of the Sunday sermon on the Great Commission, a newcomer remarks, "Who are we to say Christianity is better than any other religion? I think the essence of Jesus' teaching is love, the same as all religions, not telling other people how to live or believe." The rest of the group fidgets awkwardly, but says nothing. How do you respond?

Columbo Questions:

____

____

____

Scenario 3: The Bible

The Scene: You're riding the university shuttle with a friend who notices a Bible in your backpack. "I've read the Bible before," he says. "It's got some interesting stories, but people take it too seriously. It was only written by men, after all, and men make mistakes." You try to recall the points your pastor made a few weeks before about the Bible's inspiration, but come up empty-handed. What do you say?

Columbo Questions:

____

____

____

AMBASSADOR SKILLS

Sometimes this first Columbo question is directed at a specific statement or topic of conversation. Other times, the question can be more open-ended to make friendly conversation and draw the other person out a bit. As the discussion continues, gently guide the dialogue (if you can) into a more spiritually productive direction with additional questions.

REFLECT FOR A MOMENT

Learning how to ask this first question is the first step in our game plan and your key to productive conversations, as people frequently don't know what they mean by the things they say, as strange as that may sound. Often they're just repeating slogans, so their statements, questions, opinions, or points of view are so muddled that it's impossible to proceed in the conversation without getting clarification. Asking some form of the question "What do you mean by that?" is the simplest way to clear up the confusion while also giving you time to size up the situation and gather your own thoughts.

INTERACTIVE STUDY

The Real World

Objective: Learn to use the first Columbo question, "What do you mean by that?" to gather information and move the conversation in a productive direction.

Think for a moment about three challenges to Christianity you have heard in the last year. Describe each view in one sentence. (1 minute)

Challenge

____

____

Challenge

____

____

Challenge

____

____

With a partner, assume the roles of challenger and defender so that the defender (the Christian) can practice using the Columbo question. What specific questions would you use to gather information or seek clarification of the challenge? After two minutes, switch roles.

VI. WHAT MAIN POINTS WERE COVERED IN THIS SESSION?

A. First, we talked about that missing piece that sometimes makes conversations so difficult—that bridge from the content to the conversation.

B. Second, we learned the value of using the tactical approach when discussing Christianity.

1. Tactics help you manage the conversation by getting you into the driver's seat and keeping you there.
2. Tactics help you maneuver effectively in the face of opposition.
3. Tactics help your conversations seem more like diplomacy than D-Day.

C. Next, we defined tactics and distinguished them from strategy.

1. Strategy involves the *big picture,* which, in our case, means the content, information, and reasons why someone should believe Christianity is true.
2. Tactics, by contrast, involve the *details of maneuvering* in conversation.

D. Fourth, we learned some of the dangers of using tactics.

1. Tactics are not tricks, slick ruses, or clever ploys that belittle or humiliate the non-Christian.
2. Tactics are used to gain a footing, to maneuver, and to exploit another person's bad thinking so you can guide him to truth.

E. Fifth, I suggested a modified goal for your conversations.

1. Focus on "gardening" instead of on trying to close the deal.
2. Try to "put a stone in their shoe," aiming to take smaller steps to move someone toward the Lord.

F. Finally, I introduced you to the game plan itself: the Columbo tactic.

1. Columbo is a disarming way to take the initiative using carefully selected questions to productively advance the conversation.
2. The Columbo tactic is advantageous because questions are:
   a. Excellent conversation starters.
   b. Interactive by nature, inviting others to participate in dialogue.
   c. Neutral, protecting you from just "preaching."

d. Helpful ways to make headway without stating your case.
e. Able to buy you valuable time.
f. Essential to keeping you in the driver's seat of the conversation.

3. The first step of the game plan is to gather information with the question "What do you mean by that?" (or some variation).
   a. This question allows a person to clarify his meaning so you don't misunderstand or misrepresent him.
   b. This question also forces the other person to think more carefully about his exact meaning.
4. In the next session, you'll learn another powerful use of the Columbo tactic, the second step in your game plan: reversing the burden of proof.

INTERACTIVE STUDY

Self-Assessment

Try to answer the following questions without using your notes.

1. What is the missing piece in our approach to sharing with others?
   - We are missing a ______________ from the ______________ to the ____________________________.

2. What are the three essential qualities of a good ambassador?
   - __________________: an ______________________________ mind.
   - __________________: an ______________________________ method.
   - __________________: an ______________________________ manner.

3. What insight suggests that we change our approach to evangelism?
   - Before there can be any __________________, there must always be a season of ______________________________________.

4. What is the modified goal for our conversations about Christ?
   - Instead of trying to ______________________, we are going to try to put a ______________________.

5. What is the difference between tactics and strategy?
   - Strategy involves the ______________.
   - Tactics involve the ______________.

6. Finish these sentences:
   - Tactics are not ______________________.
   - Tactics are not meant to ______________________.

7. What are good tactics meant to accomplish?
   - Tactics are clever ways to ________ to get a footing or an ______________ in a conversation.
   - Tactics are meant to exploit another's ______________ for the purpose of guiding him to ____________.

8. The key to the Columbo tactic is using carefully selected ______________ to productively ________ the conversation.

9. Give some of the advantages to using the Columbo tactic.
   - Questions are excellent ________________ starters.
   - Questions are ____________ by nature, inviting others to participate in dialogue.
   - Questions are ______________; there is no "preaching" involved.
   - You can make headway without actually ______________ your case.
   - Questions can buy you valuable ____________.
   - Questions keep you in the __________________ of the conversation.

10. The first application of Columbo is to gather _______________ and employs some form of the question "____?"

Self-Assessment with Answers

1. What is the missing piece in our approach to sharing with others?
   - We are missing a *bridge* from the *content* to the *conversation.*

2. What are the three essential qualities of a good ambassador?
   - Knowledge: an accurately informed mind.
   - Wisdom: an artful method.
   - Character: an attractive manner.

3. What insight suggests that we change our approach to evangelism?
   - Before there can be any *harvest*, there must always be a season of *gardening.*

4. What is the modified goal for our conversations about Christ?
   - Instead of trying to *close the deal*, we are going to try to put a *stone in their shoe.*

5. What is the difference between tactics and strategy?
   - Strategy involves the *big picture.*
   - Tactics involve the *details of engagement.*

6. Finish these sentences:
   - Tactics are not *tricks, slick ruses, or clever ploys.*
   - Tactics are not meant to *belittle or humiliate the non-Christian.*

7. What are good tactics meant to accomplish?
   - Tactics are clever ways to *maneuver* to get a footing or an *appropriate advantage* in a conversation.
   - Tactics are meant to exploit another's *bad thinking* for the purpose of guiding him to *truth.*

8. The key to the Columbo tactic is using carefully selected *questions* to productively *advance* the conversation.

9. Give some of the advantages to using the Columbo tactic.
   - Questions are excellent *conversation* starters.
   - Questions are *interactive* by nature, inviting others to participate in dialogue.
   - Questions are *neutral*; there is no "preaching" involved.
   - You can make headway without actually *stating* your case.
   - Questions can buy you valuable *time.*
   - Questions keep you in the *driver's seat* of the conversation.

10. The first application of Columbo is to gather *information* and employs some form of the question *"What do you mean by that?"*

GOING DEEPER: Information for Self-Study

1. This week, make it a point to enter into conversations with others using some form of the question "What do you mean by that?" Follow Hugh Hewitt's rule and ask at least half a dozen questions in every conversation. You'll be amazed at how much you'll learn and how enjoyable the interaction can be when none of the pressure is on you. If you are studying the tactical game plan as part of a group, be prepared to share your experiences with others when you meet for session 2.

2. Review the self-assessment exercise above so you'll be able to answer all the questions without the word prompts. At the beginning of the next class, you'll be given an exercise to demonstrate your mastery of these questions. Be prepared.

3. Skim over the next lesson in this workbook before the next class to prepare yourself for the session. This simple preview will help you understand the material when you cover it in your next meeting.

FOOD FOR THOUGHT

Good Questions Bring Clarity . . .

"What do you mean by that?" is an important question that forces the other person to make sense of his own objections.

For example, a common challenge to the authority of the Bible is, "The Bible was only written by men." Yes, the Bible was written by men, of course. We agree on that. But something else is implied by the word "only." This needs to be fleshed out for clarification, and your question helps accomplish that. For example, does the challenger mean that man is incapable of writing something true or without error? (This is a strong claim with obvious counterexamples. In fact, he takes his own view about the Bible's fallibility to be true and without error.) Or does he mean that if God exists, He could not ensure that human beings would write what He wanted them to write? (This is also a strong claim that borders on the preposterous.)

Other times, the first Columbo question serves merely to clarify an issue, which often is all that's needed to parry an objection.

For example, when someone says, "Who are you to say?" or "Don't force your morality on me," you can ask what she means. Does she mean that you don't have a right to speak your opinion? Or that you can express your opinion as long as you don't think it's correct? In what way does she think you were "forcing" your opinion on her? If you're stating your opinion and arguing for it (just as she is doing), what exactly is her objection to that? If she's bothered because you insist your own view is correct, isn't she doing exactly the same thing regarding her point of view?

. . . Toward More Subversive Questioning

Let's consider the usefulness of the Columbo tactic in a specific example—say, when someone raises the issue of church and state separation when you make a political point as a Christian. In their mind, political opinions that are motivated by religious or moral convictions somehow create a breach in the wall of separation between church and state. But this isn't accurate. The nonestablishment clause of the First Amendment restricts the government, not the citizens.

If someone were to invoke the church-state separation challenge, you could simply ask him what he means by that challenge. Your Columbo tactic would look something like this: "Are you saying that Christians should have no vote, or that they should have no voice? Or do you mean that only opinions motivated by or based on atheism or secularism are legitimate? How does having a religion-based conviction automatically disqualify a person's right to speak? It seems to me that in our system, everyone is entitled to his opinion and opportunity to vote, regardless of religious conviction. Do you disagree with that?"

SESSION 2

Refining the Columbo Tactic

INTERACTIVE STUDY

Demonstrating Mastery

Try recalling the answers to the following questions without using your notes. The answers are located at the end of session 1.

1. What is the missing piece in our approach to sharing with others?
   - We are missing a ______________ from the ______________ to the ______________________________.

2. What are the three essential qualities of a good ambassador?
   - __________________: an ____________________________ mind.
   - __________________: an ____________________________ method.
   - __________________: an ____________________________ manner.

3. What insight suggests that we change our approach to evangelism?
   - Before there can be any ________________, there must always be a season of ____________________________________.

4. What is the modified goal for our conversations about Christ?
   - Instead of trying to ____________________, we are going to try to put a ____________________.

5. What is the difference between tactics and strategy?
   - Strategy involves the ____________________.
   - Tactics involve the ____________________.

6. Finish these sentences:
   - Tactics are not ____________________.
   - Tactics are not meant to ____________________.

7. What are good tactics meant to accomplish?
   - Tactics are clever ways to ____________________.
   - Tactics are meant to ____________________.

8. The key to the Columbo tactic is ____________________.

9. Give at least three advantages to using the Columbo tactic.

   a. ____________________

   b. ____________________

   c. ____________________

10. The first application of Columbo is to ____________________ and employs the question "____________________?"

INTERACTIVE STUDY

Reflect on last session's assignment. How did you use the first Columbo question to initiate conversations, gather information, or clarify a point of view? Share your experience with someone else.

I. REVIEW

A. In the last session, we covered the following:

1. The missing piece that sometimes makes conversations so difficult—that bridge from the content to the conversation.
2. The value of using a tactical approach.
    a. Tactics help you manage the conversation by putting you in the driver's seat.
    b. Tactics help you maneuver effectively in the face of opposition.
    c. Tactics make your engagements with others seem more like diplomacy than D-Day.
3. The distinction between tactics and strategy.
    a. Strategy involves the big picture.
    b. Tactics involve the actual details of maneuvering in conversation—the orderly, immediate, hands-on choreography of the particulars.
4. The danger of using tactics.
    a. Tactics are not tricks meant to belittle or humiliate non-Christians.
    b. Tactics are clever ways to gain an appropriate advantage and stay in control of the conversation.
5. Modifying our goal to do gardening, not harvesting, trying to "put a stone in their shoe."
6. Introducing the Columbo tactic.

a. The Columbo tactic allows you to take the initiative in a disarming way by using carefully selected questions to advance the conversation.
   1) Questions are a great way to start a conversation.
   2) Questions are interactive.

b. The Columbo tactic removes the need for "preaching," since you can make good headway without actually stating your case.

c. The first step of the Columbo game plan is to gather information using the question "What do you mean by that?"
   1) This clarification question provides you with important information about your friend's views.
   2) This question encourages her to think more carefully about what she means.

B. In this session, we'll do the following:

1. Examine the second use of the Columbo tactic, the second step of the game plan: reversing the burden of proof.
2. Learn how to avoid a common trap in conversations.
3. Discover what to do when you don't know what to do.
4. Learn how to use the Columbo tactic to keep you out of the "hot seat."

AMBASSADOR SKILLS

The Columbo tactic enables you to escape the charge "You're twisting my words!" When someone offers that challenge, respond by saying, "How could I twist your words by asking questions? I'm asking for clarification precisely because I don't want to twist your words. I want to understand your view, not distort it."

II. THE SECOND STEP IN THE COLUMBO GAME PLAN: REVERSING THE BURDEN OF PROOF

A. The first application of Columbo helped you understand what a person thinks; the second application—reversing the burden of proof—helps you learn why he thinks the way he does.

What is the "burden of proof"?

INTERACTIVE STUDY

Consider the following statements:

"The only rational explanation for how we got here is evolution. You can believe in creation if you want, but that's all based on your faith in the Bible."

"A fetus doesn't have self-awareness, so it's not a person. You think that a blob of cells is more important than real people who are already here? That's a religious claim you accept without proof."

"The Gospels are a bunch of stories created by early Christians to get other people to join their religion. You fundamentalists just have blind faith in your Bible stories."

Now consider the following questions or, if you're in a group, discuss them with another group member:

1. How do these statements affect your confidence? Would you shy away from answering a critic who said these things? Why?
2. What do you think the phrase "burden of proof" means?
3. Who shoulders the burden of proof in statements like these? Why?
   a. The burden of proof is the responsibility someone has to defend or give evidence for his view.
   b. The burden of proof has one cardinal rule: Whoever makes the claim bears the burden.

   c. Don't allow yourself to be thrust into a defensive position when the other person is making the claim.
4. Here's the rule: No more free rides for the nonbeliever.
   a. It isn't the Christian's responsibility to refute every story a challenger can spin or every claim he can manufacture.
   b. When your friend advances an opposing view, it's her job to defend it.
      1) Steer the burden of proof back on her shoulders, where it belongs.
      2) Make her give you her *reasons*, not just her point of view.

REFLECT FOR A MOMENT

Often, challenges to Christianity thrive on vague generalities and empty, forcefully made slogans. The burden-of-proof rule obliges a critic to go beyond mere assertions and actually give reasons for his view.

5. Let's watch this rule in action.
   a. The following dialogue occurred on a secular talk-radio station in Los Angeles when a caller disagreed with my point that the Big Bang theory provided evidence *for* God, not *against* Him. I argued that, simply put, a Big Bang needs a big "Banger."

CALLER: Well, I don't think it does, because you could start with a base of nothing, and you could say that there was nothing but an infinite, continuous moment until, eventually, one insignificant thing happened: a point happened in the nothingness. And then that point expanded, which is an extremely simple process. It requires no intelligence, so no intelligent God had to intervene. All we needed was a tiny imperfection in the perfect nothingness, and that imperfection could then expand and become variegated and increasingly complex, and soon you would have galaxies and planets.

GREG: I understand the story, and I like the way you started: "You could say that . . ." Well, that's just what you've done—you just *said* it. You've just told a story. It's one thing to "say" it. It's another thing to demonstrate it's reasonable given the evidence. That evidence shows the universe had a beginning. Now we have to explain how that beginning came to be. You can't explain it by natural law, because that was the beginning of natural law.

GREG: [*to the host*] This is a good call because it illustrates something: the tendency of people who don't like a point of view to tell a story to explain it away. But it's just a fairy tale to say, "Once upon a time there was nothing, and then something came out of nothing." It may be very easy for him to believe, but a story is not evidence.

b. Here's the takeaway: Telling a story is one thing, but giving evidence or reasons for it is another thing altogether. These tales have rhetorical power, and are effective to psychologically dislodge your confidence in what you believe. But they're nothing more than stories until they're put to the test.
   (1) It's the other person's job to defend his own view first.
   (2) It is not our job to refute it.

REFLECT FOR A MOMENT

Remember: An alternate explanation is not a refutation. It's not enough for someone to simply contradict your view by offering an alternative that appeals to her, even if it is a plausible one. That might be a legitimate first step, but she must take it further by showing why her alternate view is *more reasonable* than your view. She must shoulder the burden of proof for her own ideas, not push that burden off on you.

Reversing the burden of proof is not a way to avoid defending our own claims. When we make claims, we have to defend them with reasons too. We have a responsibility, but so do those who challenge us. That's my point.

GOING DEEPER: Information for Self-Study

There are exceptions to the burden-of-proof rule. Some beliefs reflect self-evident truths or are "properly basic" beliefs. That there are no square circles, for example, is self-evidently true and needs no defense.[11] Properly basic beliefs are those beliefs that are grounded in reasonable assumptions about reality. For example, we are under no obligation to prove our own existence or the basic reliability of our senses. Unless given evidence to the contrary, the way things appear to be probably are the way things actually are. This applies to the basic laws of logic, as well. We need them to have any form of meaningful conversation at all, and therefore are under no obligation to prove them to be true.

INTERACTIVE STUDY

Think—Pair—Share

Take a moment to reflect on the burden-of-proof concept and the role it plays in conversation. How would you explain it to another person? What is the tactical importance of understanding this concept? Find someone and rehearse with them what you've just learned. Be sure to clarify why an alternate explanation is not a refutation.

Now, with your partner, test your knowledge by deciding who bears the burden of proof in the following scenario:

JOHN: The president is so foolish. He's withholding funding for embryonic stem cell research.

JAMES: Isn't embryonic stem cell research immoral?

JOHN: You haven't been listening to those religious pro-life people, have you? They're such extremists.

JAMES: What's extreme about saying embryonic stem cell research is wrong?

JOHN: Because stem cell research would really help a lot of people.

JAMES: But doesn't stem cell research kill innocent human beings?

JOHN: You think embryos the size of the period at the end of this sentence are human beings?

JAMES: Sure, they're human beings.

JOHN: No, they're not. They're just protoplasm.

JAMES: Yes, they are. They're every bit as human as you are.

JOHN: No, they're not. They're only potentially human.

JAMES: They're already human.

JOHN: I disagree. You and I are human beings. An embryo is different.

So who bears the burden of proof?

Both are making claims. The central claims explicit at the end of the dialogue are that the embryo is not a human being (John) and that the embryo is a human being (James). Neither one is making a case for his view. They are just trading assertions and getting nowhere. Both should be asking the second Columbo question.

B. The second Columbo question is, "Now, how did you come to that conclusion?"

1. This question graciously assumes that the other person has actually reached a conclusion—that he has reasons for his view and has not merely asserted it.
   a. It will give him a chance to express his rationale, if he has one.
   b. It will also give you more material to work with in addressing his concerns.
   c. It ultimately shifts the burden of proof to the other person, which is where it belongs if he's making the claim.
2. Since many people have never thought through their views and don't know why they hold them, don't be surprised if you get a blank stare after asking this question (the "sounds of silence").
3. Alternate questions are, "Why do you say that?" or "What are your reasons for holding that view?"

AMBASSADOR SKILLS

Sometimes the simplest, most effective question you can ask someone is a variation of the question "How do you know?"

- "Why should I believe what you believe?"
- "What makes you think that's the right way to see it?"
- "I'm curious. What makes you think that's true?"
- "Why should I trust that your organization or your religious leader—the Mormon Church, Joseph Smith, the Jehovah's Witnesses—speaks for God?"

REFLECT FOR A MOMENT

Sometimes we can spend a long time helping someone carefully work through a preliminary issue without ever mentioning God, Jesus, or the Bible. This doesn't mean we aren't advancing the Kingdom, though, since this can be a form of pre-evangelism. It's always a step in the right direction when we help people learn how to discover truth. It gives them tools to assess the bigger questions that will eventually come up.

Further, when we challenge people to think carefully, we acknowledge that they bear the image of God. This affirms their intrinsic worth.

4. Consider these Columbo #2 responses to the following claims.
   a. "You can never know anything for sure."—Why should I believe that? Can you give me a good reason why I should think nothing can be known with confidence?
   b. "Morals are just an invention of culture; there are no objective moral rules."—What would be your evidence for that?
   c. "The miracles of Jesus in the Gospels were inventions of the early church."—Can you give me some of the reasons why you think that's true?

d. "The resurrection of Christ is a myth added hundreds of years after Jesus lived."—What support do you have for that idea?
e. "People are born homosexual."—What is the scientific evidence that homosexuality is genetic?
f. "The unborn may be human, but they're not persons."—What's the difference between a human and a person?

INTERACTIVE STUDY

Think—Pair—Share

Remember John and James, who disagreed about whether the embryo is a human being? Read the last portion of their dialogue again and determine what burden-of-proof questions each person could ask to make the conversation more productive.

JAMES: Sure, they're human beings.
JOHN: No, they're not. They're just protoplasm.
JAMES: Yes, they are. They're every bit as human as you are.
JOHN: No, they're not. They're only potentially human.
JAMES: They're already human.
JOHN: I disagree. You and I are human beings. An embryo is different.
JAMES: ____?
JOHN: ____?

GOING DEEPER: Information for Self-Study

Occasionally, in response to your request for reasons, a person will quip, "I guess I don't have any reasons; I just believe it." This is a remarkable admission that should not pass without you asking another question: "Why would you believe something you have no reason to think is true?"

If he says he doesn't need reasons to believe something, ask why he would believe *that.* See if he takes the bait and proceeds to give reasons why he doesn't need to give reasons.

C. Beware of the "professor's ploy."

1. Many professors are deeply committed to destroying the convictions of Christians in their classes, making remarks like "The Bible is just a bunch of fables," even if their class has nothing to do with religious issues.
2. Well-meaning believers sometimes take the challenge and attempt a head-to-head duel with the professor, but this approach is rarely successful.
3. A basic rule of engagement governs exchanges like these: The man with the microphone wins.
   a. Never attempt a frontal assault on a superior force in an entrenched position!
   b. The professor always has the strategic advantage, and he knows it.
   c. Don't get into a power play when you're out-gunned.
4. There's a better way.
   a. Don't disengage; instead, use your tactics.
   b. Raise your hand and ask, "Professor, what do you mean by that?"
   c. Next ask, "How did you reach that conclusion?" (or some variation).
   d. Make him—the teacher and the one making the claim—shoulder the burden of proof.
   e. This approach enables you to stay engaged while deftly sidestepping the power struggle.
5. The "professor's ploy" is simply his attempt to get *you* to shoulder the burden of proof when *he* has made the claim.
   a. When you ask your Columbo questions, he may assume you're a Christian and call you out saying, "You must be one of those Christians who thinks the Bible is the inspired Word of God. Okay, since I'm a fair man I'll give you a few minutes to prove that to the rest of the class. Go ahead."

   b. In one quick move, he has cleverly placed the burden of proof on you, the student, even though you didn't make the claim.
   c. Don't take the bait!
      1) You aren't the one making the claim; he is.
      2) He must defend his own view. He's the teacher, after all.
6. Here's how to respond to the "professor's ploy."
   a. When he tries to shift the burden of proof on you, calmly say, "Professor, first, you don't know what I believe because I haven't said anything about that. Second, my views don't really matter right now. You're the teacher, and you've made a claim about the Bible. I'm just trying to get clear on your meaning and also learn if you have any good reasons for it."
   b. If he gives an answer, thank him for it and either ask him another question or let it go.
7. Pressing the burden-of-proof rule takes the pressure off you, but still keeps you in the driver's seat.
   a. You don't have to be the expert on every subject.
   b. If you keep the burden on the other side when the other person is making the claim, you don't have to have all the answers.
   c. In fact, you can be effective even when you know very little if you ask the right questions.

Remember, the two most important tactical questions you can ever ask are some form of "What do you believe?" and "Why do you believe it?"

INTERACTIVE STUDY

Have you ever been cornered by someone who aggressively asserted her own view, but gave no reasons? Think how you might have responded differently if you knew then what you know now about the burden of proof.

REFLECT FOR A MOMENT

Keep in mind that the tone of these questions—"What do you mean by that?" and "How did you come to that conclusion?"—is engaging and conversational. The questions allow you to probe deeper while remaining amicable. They keep you in the driver's seat while the other person does the work.

D. Don't sweat it if you're not sure where to go next.

1. The third use of Columbo, covered in the next session, helps you make a point by using questions to either explain your own point of view, or exploit the flaws, difficulties, or problems you see in another's view.
2. Getting to the third step, however, requires insight you may not have just yet.
3. If you don't have the resources to go further or you sense the person is losing interest, don't feel compelled to force the conversation.
   a. Let the encounter die a natural death.
   b. Consider it a fruitful learning experience, nonetheless.
4. Remember, you don't have to hit home runs. You don't even have to get on base.
   a. Sometimes just getting up to bat will do.
   b. The first two Columbo questions accomplish that.

REFLECT FOR A MOMENT

In my opinion, you don't have to get to the Gospel in every encounter. Most people need time to consider what you've talked about, and that's healthy. After all, if people get to the cross too quickly, they may leave it just as quickly.

Remember, some Christians are good "closers" and some are not. Those who are consistently successful at bringing others to a decision for Christ with the simple Gospel mistakenly think it should be just as simple for everyone else. The fact is, other ambassadors have usually paved the way for them with planting, watering, and weeding (1 Cor. 3:7–8), making it possible for them to harvest with ease because the fruit is ripe.

As we learned earlier, most of us are not harvesters, but gardeners, tending the crop so that others can harvest in due season. Some Christians, aware of their difficulty in harvesting, never get into the field at all. But it's okay to garden even if someone else gets to harvest. As different members of the same Body, we each play a unique and vital role.

INTERACTIVE STUDY

The Real World Redux

Objective: To practice using the first two Columbo questions in real-world interactions and to learn how others argue against Christianity (since you'll have trouble persuading others if you can't understand what it's like to be in their shoes).

List three challenges to the Christian worldview in one-sentence statements below. These will be conversation starters in this activity.

Challenge

____

____

Challenge

____

____

Challenge

____

____

Find someone to pair up with, then choose who will be the challenger and who will be the defender. The challenger presents his challenge to Christianity, and the defender uses the first two Columbo questions ("What do you mean by that?" and "How did you come to that conclusion?") to gather information and to keep the burden of proof where it belongs. The challenger should do his best to respond as he thinks the non-Christian would. When done, switch roles.

Afterward, reflect on how the activity went. How did it feel to think like a non-Christian and to be on the receiving end of the questions? How did it feel to defend Christianity using the Columbo tactic? Did it make your job easier? Could you use this tactic in the real world?

AMBASSADOR SKILLS

Narrating the Debate

Many people you talk to will struggle when you turn the tables and ask them to provide evidence for their views. They'll try to change the subject or simply reassert their views, sometimes because they haven't thought much about the issue you're discussing. Dodging your question may be their only recourse.

It's critical you "narrate the debate" at this point. Take a moment to stop and describe to them what's going on in the conversation. This will help your friend (and others listening in) to see how she's gotten off course. You can say, "Hold on. First you made a fairly controversial statement, which I asked you to clarify and defend. So far, you haven't done that. You've just taken off in another direction. Before we move on to a new topic, can we finish this one?"

Don't let your friend get off the hook by dodging the issues. The tactical approach keeps the pressure on while keeping the conversation cordial. Encourage your friend to clarify herself. This often is the first step toward a change of mind.

E. The Columbo tactic can also help keep you out of the "hot seat."

1. Sometimes the fear of getting in over our heads is enough to keep us from saying anything at all.

2. We especially dread the possibility of some aggressive critic blasting us with arguments, opinions, or information we're not equipped to handle.
3. The Columbo tactic helps you stay in control of the conversation when you fear being overmatched by the person you're talking with.
4. When you feel overwhelmed in a conversation, buy yourself some thinking time by simply switching to fact-finding mode.
   a. Begin by slowing the pace down with, "You seem to know a lot more about this than I do. I wonder if you can slow down a bit for me since this information is new to me."
   b. Next say, "I want to understand your point, so can you carefully tell me what you believe and why you believe it?" (the first two Columbo questions).
   c. When you've heard them out say, *"Okay, now let me think about it."* Memorize this sentence, because these are magic words that get you off the hook. If you say you're going to think about it, you have no obligation to answer the challenge just then.
   d. Now you're free to work on the issue later, at your leisure, on your own, when the pressure is off.

REFLECT FOR A MOMENT

Think for a moment about how useful this approach is. Instead of trying to resist the force of another's attack, practice a little verbal aikido—just step aside and let him move forward. Give him the floor and invite him to make his case. Have him do it slowly and clearly so you fully understand his point.

When you're overwhelmed, this move to fact-finding mode takes you completely out of the hot seat. It deftly shifts control of the conversation back to you while shifting the spotlight—and the pressure—back on your challenger. You're no longer under any obligation to answer, refute, or even respond because you've already said you need to give the issue more thought.

This is easy. Essentially you're saying, "Oh, you want to beat me up? Fine with me. Just do it slowly and thoroughly." Even the most delicate, retiring, shy, bashful, skittish, timid, or reserved person can do this.

AMBASSADOR SKILLS

Asking simple, leading questions is an almost effortless way to accomplish balance. You can advance the dialogue and make use of the conversation for spiritual ends without seeming abrupt, rude, or pushy. Questions are engaging and interactive, probing yet amicable. Most important, they keep you in the driver's seat while someone else does the work.

III. WHAT MAIN POINTS WERE COVERED IN THIS SESSION?

A. First, we examined the second use of the Columbo tactic: reversing the burden of proof.

1. The burden of proof is the responsibility someone has to defend or give evidence for his view, and the person who makes the claim bears that burden.
2. It's not enough to simply give an alternate explanation.
3. The question used to reverse the burden of proof is, "How did you come to that conclusion?" (or some variation).

B. Second, we learned how to avoid the "professor's ploy," a common move to shift the burden of proof.

1. Don't allow yourself to get caught in a power play with a professor or someone like him. Instead, use your tactics.
2. Refuse to shoulder the burden of proof when you have not made the claim.

C. Third, we realized that we don't need to force a conversation.

1. We don't have to hit home runs every time we have a conversation with someone. Sometimes just getting up to bat will do.
2. The first two Columbo questions help us get in the game.

D. Fourth, we learned how to use the Columbo tactic to stay out of the hot seat.

1. When you find yourself overwhelmed, shift from argument mode to fact-finding mode.
2. Ask probing clarification questions without trying to win your case.
3. Work on the issues later, when the pressure is off, once you understand their point of view.

E. In the next session, we'll look at the final use of the Columbo tactic—using questions to make a point.

You'll also learn how to improve your Columbo skills and how to defend against the Columbo tactic when someone else uses it on you.

INTERACTIVE STUDY

Self-Assessment

Try to answer the following questions without using your notes.

1. What do we mean by the term "burden of proof"?
   - The burden of proof is the ______________________________ someone has to ______________________________ his own view.

2. What is the burden-of-proof rule?
   - The person who ______________________________ bears the burden.

3. What is the second key question of the Columbo tactic?
   - "How did you ________________________?"

4. The second Columbo question graciously assumes that the nonbeliever has actually ________________________—that he has ________ for his view and has not just ________________.

5. What is the "professor's ploy"?
   - Switching the ________________________ back onto the person who hasn't ________________________.

6. What is an easy way to stay out of the hot seat when someone is coming on strong?
   - Shift from ________________ mode to ________________ mode.
   - Say, "Carefully explain your ________ and your ________ for it, then let me ________________________."

Self-Assessment with Answers

1. What do we mean by the term "burden of proof"?
   - The burden of proof is the *responsibility* someone has to *defend* his own view.

2. What is the burden-of-proof rule?
   - The person who *makes the claim* bears the burden.

3. What is the second key question of the Columbo tactic?
   - "How did you *come to that conclusion*?"

4. This second Columbo question graciously assumes that the nonbeliever has actually *come to a conclusion*—that he has *reasons* for his view and has not just *asserted it.*

5. What is the "professor's ploy"?
   - Switching the *burden of proof* back onto the person who hasn't *made the claim.*

6. What is an easy way to stay out of the hot seat when someone is coming on strong?
   - Shift from *argument* mode to *fact-finding* mode.
   - Say, "Carefully explain your *view* and your *reasons* for it, then let me *think about it.*"

GOING DEEPER: Information for Self-Study

1. This week, take another step in developing your Columbo skills in conversation. Use questions 1 and 2 ("What do you mean by that?" and "How did you come to that conclusion?" or some variation) to begin engaging others in dialogue.

2. Introduce a friend to the two uses of the Columbo tactic that you've learned. Describe the main idea of each question and your reasons for using them. Explain to him the value of the Columbo tactic and how it can help him in conversations with others.

3. Review the self-assessment exercise above so you'll be able to answer all the questions without the prompts.

FOOD FOR THOUGHT

Jesus and Columbo

It may interest you to know that Jesus frequently went on the offensive by asking probing questions meant to challenge His opponents or trap them in their foolishness. Consider these passages, for example, and reflect on the ways you might learn from Jesus.

Luke 20:22–26; Mark 12:35–37; Luke 20:2–8; Matthew 21:28–32; John 18:22–23; Luke 7:40–42; Luke 14:1–6; Luke 10:25–37

TURNING THE TABLES

If you're placed in a situation where you suspect your convictions will be labeled intolerant, bigoted, narrow-minded, or judgmental, turn the tables. When someone asks for your personal views about a moral issue, preface your remarks with a question.

Say, "You know, this is actually a very personal question you're asking, and I'd be glad to answer. But before I do, I want to know if you consider yourself a tolerant person. Is it safe to give my opinion, or are you going to judge me for my point of view? Do you respect diverse points of view, or do you condemn others for convictions that differ from yours?" If they tell you they're tolerant, then when you give your point of view, it is going to be difficult for them to find fault without looking guilty too.

This approach is especially helpful when someone asks you what you think about homosexuality or some related issue.

This response capitalizes on the fact that there is no neutral ground in these kinds of discussions. Everybody has a point of view he thinks is right, and everybody judges at some point or another. The Christian gets pigeon-holed as the judgmental one, but everyone else is judging too. It's an inescapable consequence of believing, explicitly or implicitly, in any kind of truth.

WHEN A QUESTION IS NOT A QUESTION

We've been talking about questions you can ask to get things rolling, but sometimes a question is asked of you that is not really a question, but rather a challenge in disguise, like this one: "What gives you the right to say someone else's religion is wrong?"

I'm used to getting this response from non-Christians, but once I heard it from a fellow believer. Implicit in her question was a statement, a challenge, motivated no doubt by her own mixed feelings on the subject. What right did she, as a Christian, have to lay claim to the truth of her faith and thereby claim others were wrong?

Statement-questions like this one are hard to answer because the person's intent is not entirely clear. You're caught off guard, scratching your head. The remark was worded like a question, but you're pretty sure it wasn't one. Now what?

Often the best way to navigate this kind of situation is to simply point out that the question is confusing. Say, "I get the impression you think I've made a mistake here. Where did I go wrong?" This will force the person to rephrase her question in the form of a statement, which is precisely what you want.

As I confronted this issue, I explained that the question couldn't be taken at face value. Did she really want to talk about rights? Did she really want to know who I was to make such a claim, what my credentials were, or what authority I possessed to speak on these things? Clearly not. I wasn't laying claim to any authority, nor was I promoting my pedigree, academic or otherwise. The only "rights" I was appealing to were rational rights. I offered an argument, which stands or falls on its own merits, not on the authority of the speaker.

There's nothing magical about this move. It wasn't a one-line zinger that stopped my challenger in her tracks. I wanted her to think about what was really behind her "question." When phrased in the form of a statement, I could work with her real meaning.

The most important thing to remember about these questions is that the real statements behind them are strong claims that are open to challenge. For example, the question "What gives you the right to say someone else's religion is wrong?" can be restated as "No one is justified in claiming one religious view is truer than another"—a statement that requires a defense. And that's my point. The statement-question has power only when it remains unchallenged. If you force the implicit claim to come to the surface, the objection loses its luster and you can address the real claim lurking behind the question.

NOT QUICK ON YOUR FEET?

Maybe you don't consider yourself fast enough on your feet to keep up with someone quicker than you in an intense discussion. No problem. Don't feel under pressure to immediately answer every question asked or respond to every point made.

For tactical reasons, you may want to adopt the posture of a neutral observer, as I said earlier, and shift from argument mode to fact-finding mode.

Try saying something like this: "Interesting point. I'd like to hear more. Let me ask some questions about your view and your reasons for it so I understand you. Then let me think about it. We can talk more later." This shows you take the other person's view seriously, and it also buys you valuable time.

Ask probing questions with the Columbo tactic, but don't try to win your case just then. Take notes if you need to. Make sure you understand the challenge or the objection clearly. Then do some work on your own—maybe even enlisting others in the process—and come back prepared.

If your discussion was just part of a chance meeting, you may not be able to revisit the topic with the same person, but you'll be prepared next time the issue comes up.

This is a wonderful way to completely take the pressure off you. It's not a retreat tactic; it's just a different type of engagement. It greatly reduces your anxiety level, strengthens your own confidence, and prepares you to be more effective next time around.

SESSION 3

Perfecting the Columbo Tactic

Being able to give clear answers to these questions demonstrates your mastery of the information from the last session. Use this self-assessment exercise as a review of what you learned last time.

INTERACTIVE STUDY

Demonstrating Mastery

Try recalling the answers to the following questions without using your notes. The answers are located at the end of session 2.

1. What do we mean by the term "burden of proof"?
   - The burden of proof is the ________ someone has to ________ his own view.

2. What is the burden of proof rule?
   - The person who __________________________ bears the burden.

3. What is the second key question of the Columbo tactic?
   - "How did you ____?"

4. This second Columbo question graciously assumes that the nonbeliever has actually __________________________—that he has ________________ for his view and has not just ________________.

5. What is the "professor's ploy"?
   - Switching the ______________________ back onto the person who hasn't ______________________.

6. What is an easy way to stay out of the hot seat when someone is coming on strong?
   - Shift from ______________ mode to ______________________ mode.
   - Say, "Carefully explain your ________ and your ________ for it, then let me ______________________."

INTERACTIVE STUDY

Find someone to share the results of last week's assignment with. How did you use the first and second Columbo questions to initiate conversations, gain information, clarify a point of view, or get out of the hot seat?

I. REVIEW

A. In the last session, we covered the following:

1. First, we examined the second use of the Columbo tactic: reversing the burden of proof.
   a. The burden of proof is the responsibility someone has to defend or give evidence for his view, and the person who makes the claim bears that burden.
   b. This requires an actual defense, not just an alternate explanation.
   c. The question used to reverse the burden of proof is, "How did you come to that conclusion?"
2. Second, we learned how to avoid a trap I called the "professor's ploy."
   a. Don't allow yourself to get caught in a power play when you're outgunned; instead, use your tactics.

   b. Refuse to shoulder the burden of proof when you have not made the claim.

3. Third, we learned that we don't need to force a conversation.
   a. We don't have to hit home runs every time we have a conversation with someone. Sometimes just getting up to bat will do.
   b. The first two Columbo questions help us get in the game.
4. Fourth, we discovered how to use the Columbo tactic to get ourselves out of the hot seat.
   a. We shift from argument mode to fact-finding mode.
   b. We ask probing clarification questions without trying to win our case.
   c. Once we understand the point of view, we say, "Let me think about it," then work on the issue later, when the pressure is off.

B. In this session, we'll do the following:

1. Learn the third use of the Columbo tactic: using questions to make a point.
2. Explore specific ways to improve your Columbo skills.
3. Learn how to defend against the Columbo tactic when someone else uses it on you.

AMBASSADOR SKILLS

When someone's cherished view is at stake, it's not unusual for him to raise empty objections—objections that initially sound worthwhile but simply can't be defended once examined. Probing with questions Columbo style often reveals the lack of substance behind the bluster. Like the emperor and his new clothes, all it takes is for one person to say, "You're naked," and the game is up.

Don't settle with always being on the defensive. Go on the offensive and challenge the other person's viewpoint by asking penetrating questions. That is the key to the Columbo tactic: placing the burden of proof on your friend when he makes the claim.

II. THE THIRD STEP IN THE COLUMBO TACTIC: USING QUESTIONS TO MAKE A POINT

A. Knowing what a person believes and why he believes it—things you learned from the first two steps of the Columbo tactic—allows you to ask new questions to move you forward in the conversation. This is the final stage of Columbo.

1. The first two questions are somewhat passive.
2. The third use of Columbo is more active, helping you go on the offensive in an inoffensive way. With Columbo #3 you can use questions to:
   a. Make a point or advance your own view.
   b. Exploit a weakness or a flaw in the other person's view.
3. The first two questions of the game plan require no knowledge, since both are questions meant to gather different types of information.
4. For the third use of Columbo you need to know something specific.
   a. You need to know the point you want to make.
   b. Your point is like a target and your questions are the arrows used to hit the target.
5. One of the most powerful ways I use Columbo #3 is to enlist the help of the other person to make my own point. Here's how:
   a. First, determine the steps you need to take to make your point or arrive at your conclusion.
   b. Second, ask questions to get your friend to put as many of those steps or parts on the table so you can use them (it will be much harder for him to deny something he's already agreed to).
   c. Third, use those pieces to make your point.

B. Finding the weakness, flaw, or contradiction in a person's point of view.

1. There's no special formula for making this discovery.
2. You'll uncover it by listening carefully and then thinking about what was said.

3. Your own study on the issue using books, web sites, or something you've heard from a speaker may also tip you off to a problem.

C. The key to this step is paying close attention to the answer to the question "How did you come to that conclusion?"
   1. Are there any blatant weaknesses in the view?
   2. Do the conclusions follow from the evidence?
   3. Can you question any underlying assumptions?
   4. Is there a misstep, a non sequitur, a fallacy, or a failing of some sort?

D. Address any inconsistency you discover with a question, not a statement.

E. This step takes more practice than the others, but in time you'll improve.
   1. It requires some insight—an ability to see the flaws in the argument—which is a demanding request.
   2. It's easy to "stall out" in the beginning, so don't be surprised or discouraged.

INTERACTIVE STUDY

See if you can uncover the flaws in the common challenges below. Then suggest a question that begins to address the underlying flaw and write it down in the space provided. If you get stalled on one challenge, simply move on to the next. Don't be frustrated if the problem is not clear at first.

"You shouldn't push your morality on me."

____

____

"You're intolerant and arrogant."

____

____

"The miracles in the Bible prove it's a myth."

____

____

"Jesus was a good man and a prophet, but He wasn't God or the only savior."

____

____

"A fetus may be a human being, but it's not a person."

____

____

"How can God exist when there's so much evil in the world?"

____

____

F. Let's think about how we might respond to the above challenges.

1. When they say, "You shouldn't push your morality on me," you can ask, "Why not?"
   a. It is going to be hard for them to answer this without contradicting themselves.
   b. When they say you *shouldn't* push your morality on them, *they're* pushing their morality on *you*.
2. When they say, "You're intolerant and arrogant," you can ask, "What do you mean by that?" (Columbo #1).
   a. Asking this question flushes out their definition of *intolerant* or *arrogant*, exposing what I call the "passive-aggressive tolerance trick."
   b. Here's the way it usually looks:
      1) "You're intolerant and arrogant."
      2) "What do you mean by that?"

3) "Well, you think you're right and everyone who disagrees with you is wrong."
4) "Tell me, do you think your own views are right?" Of course he does; that's why he believes them.
5) "Help me out here. Why is it that when I think I'm right, I'm intolerant, but when you think you're right, you're just right? What am I missing?"

3. When the professor says, "The Bible is just a bunch of myths and fables," ask, "How did you come to that conclusion?"
   a. The professor has probably assumed, because of his naturalistic philosophy, that miracles are impossible. Therefore, prior to evaluating any evidence (i.e., a priori[12]), he has determined that any "historical" references to miracles are myths or fables.
   b. Since modern-day science is based on naturalistic philosophy, he thinks science has proved—instead of assumed—there are no miracles.
   c. Since science can only measure the natural world, it cannot eliminate, even in principle, the possibility of events that are supernatural.
   d. The professor has made what's known as a "category error."[13]
   e. Follow up any claim that science has proved miracles don't happen by asking, "Would you explain how the methods of science can disprove the supernatural?"
4. When they say, "That's just your interpretation," you can ask, "What do you mean by 'just'?"
   a. Your goal is to find out if they believe all interpretations are equally valid and yours is "just" another in the long line of alternatives.
   b. If this is what they believe, then you're free to interpret their words any way that then strikes your fancy, an "interpretation" that is just as good as any other.
   c. You can challenge this view by making some drastic claim—for example, by saying his remarks are racist. When he asks you where you got *that* idea, say, "Well, that's *my* interpretation of what you're saying. All interpretations are equally valid, right? Or could it be that some interpretations are better than others?"

   d. You might ask, "What makes you think I got the meaning of this Bible passage wrong?"

5. When they say, "Jesus was a good man and a prophet, but He wasn't God or the only savior," you can ask, "How could Jesus be a good man and a prophet, but be mistaken about His own identity and purpose?"
   a. If Jesus was wrong about His frequent claim that He was the unique means of salvation,[14] it then becomes difficult to call Him a good man, a prophet, or a wise religious teacher.
   b. If Jesus was not correct, then He was lying or deeply deceived—qualities we would never use to describe a good man or godly prophet.
6. When they say, "The fetus may be human, but it's not a person," you can ask, "What's the difference?"
   a. They're claiming there's a morally relevant difference between an unborn child and a toddler that justifies killing one and not the other.
   b. This is a difference they must defend, not just assert.
   c. If they offer a list of qualities for personhood, ask where they got the list. What if someone else's list has a certain skin color as a requirement for personhood (it's happened before)? Who gets to make the list that qualifies some humans as protected "persons," but not others?
7. When they ask, "How can God exist when there's so much evil in the world?" you can ask, "But if there is no God, how can we call anything evil in the first place?"
   a. The existence of evil assumes an objective standard—a scoring system, of sorts—that must be in place to distinguish good from evil.
   b. But there is no way to account for a standard of objective good—the moral rules that are violated by people who commit the evil in question—without the existence of a moral rule maker: God.[15]
   c. How do we make sense of the difference between good and evil if there is no God?

G. Sometimes you can soften your approach by first requesting clarification.

1. Begin by asking, "Can you clear this up for me?" or "Can you help me understand this?"
2. Next, offer your objection by gently challenging the belief or confronting the weakness in the argument.
3. Consider the gentle approach of the following questions.
   a. Can you clear this up for me? How could the miracles of Jesus be added to every existing handwritten copy of the New Testament circulating in the Roman world many years after they were first written?
   b. Can you help me understand this? If the Bible were "merely written by men," how could it contain fulfilled prophecies?
   c. Can you clear this up for me? How does having a "burning in the bosom" about the Book of Mormon give adequate evidence for its truth when people have similar reasons—a strong conviction from God in response to prayer—for rejecting it?
   d. Can you help me understand this? If homosexuality is truly natural, then why did nature give homosexuals bodies designed for reproductive sex with women, not men? Why would nature give desires for one type of sex but the body for another?
   e. Can you clear this up for me? If abortion is morally acceptable, on what grounds do we condemn infanticide, since the only difference between the two is the baby's location—inside the womb or out—and location seems irrelevant to the baby's value?
   f. Can you help me understand this? If there is absolutely no evidence for abiogenesis (life from nonlife—life arising initially from lifeless matter) and much evidence against it, how can we say that Darwin's theory of evolution is a fact? How does life get started in the first place to give evolution something to work with?

The following dialogue is an example of one student's gentle use of the third step in the Columbo tactic. It's found in the fine critique of evolution by Jonathan Wells, *Icons of Evolution*.[16]

TEACHER: Okay, let's start today's lesson with a quick review. Yesterday I talked about homology [how different organisms show remarkable similarity in the structure of some of their body parts]. Homologous features, such as the vertebrate limbs shown in your textbook, provide us with some of our best evidence that living things have evolved from common ancestors.

STUDENT: [*raising hand*] I know you went over this yesterday, but I'm still confused. How do we know whether features are homologous?

TEACHER: Well, if you look at vertebrate limbs, you can see that even though they're adapted to perform different functions, their bone patterns are structurally similar.

STUDENT: But you told us yesterday that even though an octopus eye is structurally similar to a human eye, the two are not homologous.

TEACHER: That's correct. Octopus and human eyes are not homologous because their common ancestor did not have such an eye.

STUDENT: So, regardless of similarity, features are not homologous unless they are inherited from a common ancestor?

TEACHER: Yes, now you're catching on.

STUDENT: [*looking puzzled*] Well, actually, I'm still confused. You say homologous features provide some of our best evidence for common ancestry. But before we can tell whether features are homologous, we have to know whether they came from a common ancestor.

TEACHER: That's right.

STUDENT: [*scratching head*] I must be missing something. It sounds as though you're saying that we know features are derived from a common ancestor because they're derived from a common ancestor. Isn't that circular reasoning?

AMBASSADOR SKILLS

Sometimes the best way to disagree with someone is not to face the issue head-on, but to use an indirect approach. Offer an alternative and invite a principled response.

- "Let me suggest an alternative and tell me if it isn't an improvement. Then you can tell me why you think your alternative is better."
- "I wouldn't characterize it that way. Here's what I think may be a better or more accurate way to look at it."
- "Have you thought about or considered another alternative?"
- "I don't think that's going to work, and here's why."
- "I'm not sure I agree with the way you put it. Think about this. . . ."

This approach shows respect for the person you disagree with. Once you understand her viewpoint, you can ask, "Do you mind if I ask a couple of questions about what you've told me?" or "Would you consider an alternative or be willing to look at another angle?" By soliciting permission to disagree, you make the encounter more amicable. You also stay in the driver's seat. Remember, the person who asks the questions controls the conversation.

III. TWO BASIC EXECUTIONS OF THE COLUMBO TACTIC

A. The first approach is the apparently harmless method of Lieutenant Columbo himself—halting, head scratching, and bumbling.

   1. You can use a number of phrases to introduce questions that soften your challenge, such as:

      a. "I'm just curious . . ."

      b. "Help me out because I'm trying to understand you on this . . ."

c. "I'm a little confused on something . . ."
d. "Maybe you can clear this up for me . . ."
e. "Something about this thing bothers me . . ."
f. "Maybe I'm missing something . . ."

2. This style is best used in a college classroom or with a group of people you don't know.

B. The second approach is more confrontational and aggressive.

1. This technique is similar to that used by a lawyer in a courtroom.
2. The important rule in this approach is that a lawyer never asks a question he doesn't know the answer to.
   a. When I use the Columbo tactic aggressively, I have a goal in mind.
   b. I ask specific questions that legitimately challenge the other person's view.

IV. IMPROVE YOUR COLUMBO SKILLS WITH THREE STEPS: ANTICIPATE, REFLECT, AND PRACTICE

A. Initially, you will not be quick on your feet with responses like the ones above.

1. Your best ideas will often come afterward, when the pressure is off.
2. This is the perfect time to focus on improving your technique.

B. First, try to anticipate objections and think of questions in advance.

1. Work on an issue or question that has stumped you in the past.
   a. Brainstorm straightforward response questions that will put you in the driver's seat of those conversations.
   b. Remember that a question mark is shaped like a fishhook—you want to use questions like a hook.
2. Advance preparation takes work, but is really effective. The next time you're asked those particular questions, you'll have responses at your fingertips.

C. Second, after you've had an encounter, reflect on how you might have done better.

1. After each conversation, take a few moments for self-assessment.
    a. Think about questions you might have asked.
    b. Consider how you could have phrased questions more effectively or maneuvered through the conversation differently.
    c. With the pressure off, other alternatives may occur to you.
    d. Write down your thoughts and review them later.
2. This kind of assessment is not hard and can be a lot of fun.
    a. It prepares you for your next opportunity.
    b. It puts new ideas at your fingertips that you can use next time around.
    c. It becomes second nature when you get into the routine.

D. When you think of a new idea or approach, practice the questions—and possible rejoinders—out loud.

1. Practice increases your practical experience—it places you in the actual dialogue, yet in a safe environment.
    a. Anticipate the turns your new tack might take and how you would respond to possible rejoinders.
    b. Role-play it with a friend.
2. Practice prepares you for actual encounters.
    a. If you practice in advance, when these issues come up you'll be ready.
    b. This really works because when you face the challenge in the future you'll have already rehearsed your response.

Remember: It's not enough to prepare. You also need to step out of your comfort zone a little and engage. Interacting with others face-to-face is the most effective way to improve your abilities, and now you have a game plan to make that much easier.

AMBASSADOR SKILLS

Always try to anticipate the counterarguments the other person might raise. Take these rejoinders seriously, state them fairly and clearly—even convincingly—then learn in advance how to deal with them. This approach prepares you for objections before they come up. It's as if you're saying, "I know what you're thinking, and it's not going to work. Here's why."

INTERACTIVE STUDY

The Real World

If you don't anticipate objections, it will be harder to handle them when they come up. Think of one statement you've heard that opposes Christianity or Christians. Try to put yourself in the shoes of the one objecting. Jot down at least two reasons you think that person might give for his challenge.

The Challenge

____

____

Reason #1:

____

____

Reason #2:

____

____

In your mind, engage in an improvised dialogue. Try to present both sides of the dialogue as well as possible. How did it feel to be in "the other person's shoes," opposing Christianity? Was it difficult? Did it help you to better understand your non-Christian friends?

AMBASSADOR SKILLS

Character Check

Once you learn the Columbo tactic, you'll discover how ill-equipped other people are to answer for their own views. It's tempting, once you see this happen, to begin to take pleasure in another's failings. Therefore, take care to show concern for the other person. Establish common ground whenever possible by affirming points of agreement. Encourage the other person to think further on the subject if she doesn't have a satisfactory answer. Assume the same best intentions you would like others to assume about you when you're the one being challenged.

V. HOW TO DEFEND AGAINST THE COLUMBO TACTIC WHEN IT'S USED AGAINST YOU

A. Sometimes your friend will use the Columbo Tactic on you.

1. This shouldn't be a problem with Columbo #1 or Columbo #2. You should be able to clearly explain your own views and your reasons for them.
2. It could be a problem, though, if she uses Columbo #3 to go on the offensive and tries to trap you with your own answers.

B. Protect yourself with these two steps.

1. First, stop the advance.
    a. Don't let your friend set you up with leading questions.
    b. Politely respond by saying, "I'd rather not answer questions right now. I want to know what *you* think."
2. Second, regain control.
    a. Ask your friend to change her approach. This takes her tactical advantage away from her, yet still allows her to make her point.
    b. Say, "It sounds like you're asking questions in order to make a point. Instead, could you simply state your point clearly so I understand it?"
    c. Once you're clear on the point, you may want to use your hot-seat maneuver: "Let me think a bit about what you said and then get back to you."

AMBASSADOR SKILLS

The advantage of using Columbo #3 is not having to assert something you want someone else to believe in. You aren't taking the burden of proof on yourself. Instead, your questions make the point for you. This accomplishes your goal in an entirely different—and often much more powerful—way.

VI. WHAT MAIN POINTS DID WE COVER IN THIS SESSION?

A. First, we looked at the third use of the Columbo tactic: using questions to make a point. You may want to use #3 to advance your own view or to exploit a weakness or a flaw in the other's view.

1. Use questions to get your friend to put the "pieces" on the table that you need to make your point with.

2. To find the flaw, listen carefully to the reasons given to the second Columbo question, "How did you come to that conclusion?" Ask yourself if the conclusion follows from the evidence.
3. Point out errors with questions, rather than statements, if you can.

B. Second, you learned three specific ways to improve your Columbo skills.

1. Anticipate objections and think of questions in advance.
2. Reflect afterward on questions you might have asked.
3. Practice new questions—and potential responses—out loud.

C. Third, you learned how to defend yourself when someone uses Columbo #3 against you.

1. First, stop the advance by politely deflecting the questions your friend is using to advance her own point.
2. Second, regain control by asking her to make her point directly and give reasons for it so you can further consider her view.

D. In the next session, you will learn a powerful new maneuver: the Suicide tactic.

INTERACTIVE STUDY

Self-Assessment

Try to answer the following questions without using your notes.

1. The third application of the Columbo tactic is to use questions to ________ ________________.

2. You may want to advance ________________________________.

3. You may also use questions to __________ a weakness or __________ in the other person's views.

4. There is no special formula for finding the flaw. Just ________ carefully, then ________ about what's been said.

5. The key to finding the flaw is to pay ______________ to the answer your friend gives to ______________. Do his conclusions follow from his evidence?

6. List three specific ways to improve your Columbo skills.
   - ________ objections and think of questions in advance.
   - ________ on questions you might have asked.
   - ________ new questions—and potential responses—out loud.

7. List two steps to defend yourself against the Columbo tactic.
   - First, ________ the ________. Politely refuse to ________ his leading questions.
   - Second, regain control by asking him to simply ______________ and his ________ for it.

Self-Assessment with Answers

1. The third application of Columbo is to use questions to *make a point.*

2. You may want to advance *your own view.*

3. You may also use questions to *exploit* a weakness or *flaw* in the other person's views.

4. There is no special formula for finding the flaw. Just *listen* carefully, then *think* about what's been said.

5. The key to finding the flaw is to pay *close attention* to the answer your friend gives to *question two*. Do his conclusions follow from his evidence?

6. List three specific ways to improve your Columbo skills.
   - *Anticipate* objections and think of questions in advance.
   - *Reflect* on questions you might have asked.
   - *Practice* new questions—and potential responses—out loud.

7. List two steps to defend yourself against the Columbo tactic.
   - First, *stop* the *advance*. Politely *refuse to answer* his leading questions.
   - Second, regain control by asking him to simply *state his point* and his *reasons* for it.

GOING DEEPER: Information for Self-Study

1. This week, look for opportunities to hone your Columbo skills. Use the first two questions, "What do you mean by that?" and "How did you come to that conclusion?" to navigate in conversations. If you feel comfortable, use further questions to advance your own views or to gently challenge points of weakness you see in the other's view. If you're stumped, let the issue go for the time being and brainstorm possible responses later with a fellow believer. Be prepared to share your experiences during the next session if you're studying in a group.

2. Introduce a few friends to the three uses of the Columbo tactic. Describe the main idea of each question and your reasons for using them. Explain how they can improve their Columbo skills and defend against Columbo when someone uses it on them.

3. Review the self-assessment exercise above so you will be able to answer all the questions without the prompts.

FOOD FOR THOUGHT

Sheepish in Seattle

Once in a restaurant in Seattle, I got into a chat about religion with the waitress who was serving my table. My general comments were met with an approving nod until I said, "When it comes to religion, people believe a lot of foolish things." Then a shadow of disapproval crossed her face.

"That's oppressive, not letting people believe what they want to believe," she said.

Now, much can be said about this simple remark. For example, notice how she felt that just challenging a view was a threat to personal liberty, a "forcing" of my beliefs on others. I ignored that problem, though, and zeroed in on a more fundamental flaw. I asked a simple question—a variation of the first Columbo question.

"So, are you saying I'm wrong?"

She balked, realizing she was about to commit the same error she'd just accused me of making. "No, I'm not saying you're wrong. I'm just trying to understand your view."

I chuckled in a good-natured way. "Be honest; admit it. You think I'm wrong. If you don't think I'm wrong, then why are you correcting me? If you do think I'm wrong, then why are you 'oppressing' me?"

It was clear that she believed some people could be wrong—me, in this case. Like many who espouse this confused sense of tolerance, the waitress couldn't play by her own rules. Mine was a simple question that gently boxed her in.

After this, she stammered for a moment and then replied, "All religions are basically the same, after all." Notice that this comment had little to do with my original question. It was a parry—a stock retort. But she had just made a claim, and now it was her job to defend it.

"All religions are basically the same? In what way?" I asked.

This question had a remarkable effect on her. Her jaw fell slack, and her face went blank. She didn't know what to say. She'd obviously never looked closely at other religions. If she had, she would have known they are worlds apart. Why would she have made this claim, then? I suspect she had gotten away with it many times before.

"Consider this," I said. "Either Jesus is the Messiah or He isn't, right?" She nodded. So far, so good.

"If He isn't the Messiah," I continued, "then the Christians are wrong. If He is the Messiah, then the Jews are wrong. So, one way or another, somebody's right and somebody's wrong. Everyone can't be right at the same time, can they?"

After stumbling around a bit, the waitress offered a different diversion. "Well, no one can ever know the truth about religion."

This is another assertion that should never go unchallenged, so I calmly asked, "Why would you believe that?"

The turn-about caught her by surprise. She was used to *asking* this question, not *answering* it, and she wasn't prepared for the role change.

I waited patiently, not breaking the silence, not letting her off the hook. Finally, she ventured: "But the Bible has been changed and retranslated so many times over the centuries."

This was another dodge. It had nothing to do with the issue. Even if the Bible vanished from the face of the earth, some knowledge of God would still be possible, it seemed, at least in principle.

But I chose a different tack. "Oh? Have you actually studied the transmission of the ancient documents of the text of the Bible?"

Once again, the question stalled her. She couldn't defend her own assertion. "No, I've never studied it," she said. This was a remarkable admission, given her confident contention just moments before, but she didn't seem the least bit bothered.

It would have been impolite to say what I was thinking—"Then what you're saying is you're sure about something you really know nothing about." Instead, I simply said I'd studied Bible transmission enough to know that the academic results were in, and there was no reason to believe the Bible had been corrupted in the way she thought.

One by one, her options evaporated and she began to get uncomfortable. "I feel like you're backing me into a corner," she complained.

I wasn't trying to bully her intellectually, but rather challenge her politely with fair questions. She was beginning to feel trapped because that's what careful questioning does: By eliminating foolish options, it forces a person down the narrow corridor of truth.

Note what happened here. I said some people are foolish in their thinking on spiritual matters, and she responded by saying mine was an oppressive view. She then proved my point by serving up her standard menu of muddled challenges. With each claim she made, I responded with a question.

She was speechless not because I was clever, but because, I suspect, she had never before been challenged to answer for her own claims. I asked why I should swallow any of this, and she complained she was being cornered.

SESSION 4

The Suicide Tactic

INTERACTIVE STUDY

Demonstrating Mastery

Try recalling the answers to the following questions without using your notes. The answers are located at the end of session 3.

1. What is the third application of the Columbo tactic?
2. What are the key ways of finding a flaw in the other person's view?
3. List three specific ways to improve your Columbo skills.
4. List two steps to defend against Columbo.

INTERACTIVE STUDY

Find someone to share last session's assignment with. How did you use the Columbo tactic to expose a weakness or a flaw in someone's view? How did they respond? What friends did you introduce to the Columbo tactic? What did they think of it?

I. REVIEW

A. In the last session, we covered the following:

1. First, we learned how to employ the third use of the Columbo tactic: using

questions to make a point. We also learned some ways to discover a weakness or a flaw in another person's view.

   a. Listen carefully and think about what has been said.
   b. Pay close attention to the reasons given to Columbo #2, "How did you come to that conclusion?" and ask yourself if the conclusions follow from the evidence.
   c. Point out errors with questions rather than statements.

2. Second, we learned three steps to improve your Columbo skills.
   a. Anticipate objections and think of questions in advance.
   b. Reflect afterward on questions you might have asked.
   c. Practice your questions—and possible rejoinders—out loud by yourself or with someone else.
3. Third, we learned how to defend when the Columbo tactic is being used against us.
   a. Stop the advance by politely saying, "I'd rather not answer questions. I want to know what you think."
   b. Regain control by saying, "Why don't you state your point clearly so I don't misunderstand it, along with your specific reasons for holding this view? Then let me think about it."

B. In this session, you'll learn the Suicide tactic.

1. We'll cover the basics of self-refuting claims.
2. You'll learn how to recognize when someone's view self-destructs.
3. You'll see how specific popular ideas commit suicide and learn how to respond to them.
4. Finally, I'll show you a unique variation of the Suicide tactic I call "sibling rivalry."

II. THE SUICIDE TACTIC

A. The Suicide tactic takes advantage of the tendency many erroneous points of view have to self-destruct.

1. These self-destructive views are commonly called "self-refuting statements."
2. These views defeat themselves all on their own. All you need to do is point that out.
3. For example, consider this dialogue I saw once in a *Peanuts* cartoon.

> SALLY: No! That's my new philosophy. I don't care what anyone says, the answer is No!
>
> CHARLIE BROWN: That's your new philosophy, huh?
>
> SALLY: Yes! I mean, No! [*pause*] You've ruined my new philosophy.

4. Statements that commit suicide have within them the seeds of their own destruction.
   a. "I cannot speak a word in English" is self-refuting when spoken in English.
   b. "There are no sentences more than five words in length" is a sentence that has more than five words.
   c. "You can't know anything for sure" is a truth skeptics are pretty sure about.

GOING DEEPER: Information for Self-Study

Philosopher J. P. Moreland points out that every statement is about something.[17] For example, the sentence "Dogs have fleas" is about dogs. Sometimes statements include themselves in what they refer to. The statement "All English sentences are short" is about all English sentences, including itself. When a statement fails to satisfy its own criteria of validity, it's self-refuting. It can't possibly be true.

Suicidal statements cannot satisfy their own standard. This is why the minute someone utters them, they become false. Even when such statements initially appear true, they are still false.

This holds true for all self-refuting statements. If the exact same reasons used against your view also defeat the reasons themselves, then the view is self-defeating; it commits suicide. This doesn't mean your own view is sound, only that the self-refuting challenge against it cannot succeed. The person using such arguments can't even recommend his own advice. For example, when someone says, "You shouldn't make moral judgments," he is making a moral judgment (the word *shouldn't* is your clue).

REFLECT FOR A MOMENT

Even God Himself can't cause self-refuting statements to be true. These kinds of statements are irrational, and since rationality is part of God's essential character, He cannot violate His nature and make contradictory statements become true. This is not a limitation on God's power in any way, because power is not the relevant factor here: no amount of raw power can make a contradictory statement true. Suicidal ideas, therefore, are false by necessity. They can't be true in any possible world.

B. Here is why the Suicide tactic works.

1. The Suicide tactic works because it trades on a fundamental rule of logic: the law of noncontradiction.
   a. The law of noncontradiction states that two contradictory statements cannot be true at the same time.
   b. *A* cannot be non-*A* at the same time, in the same way.
2. All suicidal views express or entail contradictions.
   a. They make two different claims at odds with each other.
   b. The contradictions—"*A* is the case" and "*A* is not the case" may be explicit or implicit.
      1) Explicit contradictions are usually obvious.

(a) "I never, never repeat a word. Never." The contradiction: I don't repeat words. I just repeated words.

(b) "There are no absolutes." Contradiction: There are no absolutes. This is an absolute.

(c) "This page intentionally left blank." Contradiction: This page is blank. This page is not blank.

(d) "I used to believe in reincarnation. But that was in a former life." Contradiction: I don't believe in reincarnation. I do believe in reincarnation.

(e) "I'll give you three good reasons you can't use logic to find truth." Contradiction: He wants to use logic to disprove the use of logic.

2) Implicit contradictions are often hidden and sometimes require further reflection to see.

(a) "My brother is an only child." Contradiction: My brother has a sibling (me). My brother has no siblings.

(b) "I never tell the truth." Contradiction: It's true that I never tell the truth.

(c) "Always go to other people's funerals; otherwise they won't go to yours." —Yogi Berra. Contradiction: If you don't go to a person's funeral, that person will somehow decide, after death, not to go to yours.

(d) "Ask me about my vow of silence." Contradiction: I've taken a vow of silence. Let me tell you about it.

3) Sometimes suicide is subtler.

(a) Radio caller: "You shouldn't be correcting Christian teachers publicly on the radio." (Then why is he calling my radio program to correct me in public?)

(b) "You shouldn't force your morality on me." (Why not? Are you telling me it is wrong to say that other people are wrong?)

(c) Conversation with Gil, the physical therapist:

GIL: Greg, you Christians are always judging other people. It's wrong for you to judge others.

GREG: Then why are you judging me?

GIL: Hmm . . . Okay. [*He was regrouping.*] It's all right to judge, as long as you don't try to force your morality on other people.

GREG: Is that your morality? [*He nods.*] Then why are you forcing it on me?

GIL: It's not fair! There's no way I can say it so it sounds right. [*He thought I was playing a word trick on him.*]

GREG: It doesn't sound right because it isn't right. It's self-refuting.

GIL: Now you've got me all confused.

GREG: [*Jokingly*] No, you were confused when you started. You just now realized it.

AMBASSADOR SKILLS

What's in a name? Plenty. A person's name is one of the sweetest sounds to his ears. Keep this in mind when conversations begin to get hostile or combative with someone you have just met. At the very first sign of tension, pause and ask the person his name. Then use it in a friendly manner as you continue. It can really help take the edge off.

REFLECT FOR A MOMENT

The Suicide and Columbo tactics work well together. As you pay attention to a person's viewpoint and notice that her view commits suicide, point it out with a Columbo question.

C. To recognize a point that commits suicide, take the following steps:

1. First, identify the basic premise, conviction, or claim. It's not always obvious.
2. Next, ask yourself if the claim undermines itself.
    a. Does the statement satisfy its own requirements?
    b. Is there an internal contradiction?
    c. Can the idea be stated in the form "X is the case" and "X is not the case" at the same time? If so, it commits suicide.

INTERACTIVE STUDY

Work through the challenges below to identify their flaws. Each of them falls prey to the Suicide tactic. Can you find the self-refutation?

Anthropology professor to Christian student: "You shouldn't be a missionary because it's wrong to try to change other people's religious beliefs."

"All religions are equally true and valid."

"You can only know what has been proven by science."

"There is no truth."

"It's wrong to try to change other people's religious beliefs."

- This statement claims it is wrong to change other people's religious beliefs, yet the statement itself is meant to change someone's religious belief—the Christian belief in the Great Commission.
- Contradiction: It's wrong to change people's religious beliefs. It's not wrong to change people's religious beliefs.

"All religions are equally true and valid."

- If all religions are true, then Christianity is true and valid, yet an essential claim of Christianity is that all other religions are false, taken as a whole.
- Either Christianity is true and others are false, or others are true and Christianity is false.
- Either way, all religions can't be true.[18]
- Contradiction: All religions are true. All religions are not true.

"You can only know what has been proven by science."

- This statement makes a truth claim—a claim that the speaker implies he knows.
- It self-destructs because scientific proofs and experiments can't teach us that science is the only way to learn truth.
- Contradiction: Only science can teach us what we know. This is something we know that science didn't teach us.

AMBASSADOR SKILLS

Sometimes people don't see contradictions staring them in the face. When that happens, gently point them out. Other times they miss a contradiction because they don't have the information they need, like with the claim that all religions lead to God. Some people may not see the problem with religious pluralism because they don't know that Jesus claimed to be the only true way to the Father (John 14:6). In such cases, you'll have to give them the correct information before they'll see the conflict.

REFLECT FOR A MOMENT

When approaching the "science is the only source of truth" problem, use the first Columbo question. Ask, "Am I to take that statement as mere feeling, personal preference, or fact?" If the person takes it as fact, then he needs to defend how he knows it to be so. Facts are knowable only through scientific proof—in his view—so to prove as fact that science is the only source of truth, he must provide scientific evidence for it. As it turns out, this claim is not a fact of science, but a philosophical claim about science that can't actually be known, according to this approach.[19]

"There is no truth."

- This is a postmodern claim that ultimately denies we can know anything about the world "out there."
- Postmodernism is a community-based relativism that claims all "truth"—all perception of reality—is "constructed" by one's linguistic community, and that each account of "reality" is equally and actually true for those who believe it.
- In this view, there is no truth in the sense that most of us use the word—an accurate understanding of the way the world really is.
- Contradiction: We cannot know truth. We know this to be true. It is true that there is no truth.

REFLECT FOR A MOMENT

Careful postmodernists will deny they are making claims about how the world actually is. But how, then, are we to take their own statements? In spite of their protests, postmodernists make sweeping claims about knowledge itself, and not just about the knowledge within their own linguistic communities. This is why postmodernism commits suicide.

AMBASSADOR SKILLS

Here is how the Suicide tactic worked out for me in a debate with Dr. Marv Meyer at Chapman University titled "Is Truth True?" I defended the resolve, "Objective truth exists and can be known." Dr. Meyer took the opposing view, arguing that nothing can be known, which is a contradiction (he knows he can't know?). Dr. Meyer's efforts were doomed to failure from the start. By merely showing up to defend this view, he implicitly acknowledged that he thought his own ideas were true, effectively conceding my claim before he even said a word. Further, every vote for Dr. Meyer was a vote that his view was objectively true and mine was false. In other words, every vote for Meyer was really a vote for me.

INTERACTIVE STUDY

Stop the Suicide

How would you use questions (Columbo #3) to expose the suicidal tendencies of the following self-refuting statements?

- "It's wrong to condemn anybody for anything."
- "Everyone's view is a product of his own prejudices."
- "God doesn't take sides."
- "You are what you eat."
- "The world is an illusion [*Maya*], and we're each part of the illusion."
- "The Bible could not have been inspired by God, because men wrote it and men make mistakes."
- "God can't exist because there's so much evil in the world."
- "God used Darwinian evolution to design the world."

AMBASSADOR SKILLS

One goal of the Suicide tactic is to show the ambiguities—even double standards—in the claims of others. When someone says "There is no truth," it's clear he believes some truths, just not others. When he says, "It's wrong for you to push your morality on others," he can't think it's always wrong or he wouldn't be doing it to you just then. The Suicide tactic forces the other person to address this inconsistency. How does he know what's true and what's false? Under what circumstances might we legitimately "force" morality on someone?

GOING DEEPER: Information for Self-Study

I analyze most of the challenges listed above at the end of the chapter in "Food for Thought: Mass 'Suicide,'" but I discuss a few of them in detail below.

"The world is an illusion, and we're each part of the illusion." This is a belief of some Hindu sects that say all of "objective reality" is really just an illusion. But if we are part of an illusion, how can we know that's true? Can members of a dream know they're in a dream? Does Charlie Brown know he's a cartoon character? This Hindu concept that the world is an illusion contradicts the idea that I can know I'm part of an illusion. Therefore, this central doctrine self-destructs.

"God doesn't take sides." When someone says God doesn't take sides, she thinks that this is the view God Himself holds. In a way, this is just another way of stating that God would be on her side on the issue of God taking sides, which contradicts her statement.

"God can't exist because there's so much evil in the world." When we hear this challenge, it is important that we ask what the person means by "evil." Don't let her give you examples (murder, rape, torture, etc.). Instead, ask what makes those things *intrinsically* bad in the first place. Why would we call them evil instead of good? At its core, the existence of evil implies an objective moral standard of perfection that has in some way been violated. As C. S. Lewis once observed, "A man does not call something crooked unless he has some idea of a straight line."[20] Only God can be the true standard of moral perfection. Since God's existence is necessary to make the notion of evil intelligible, the existence of evil cannot be invoked as a proof that God does not exist. It proves just the opposite.

D. Let's examine "sibling rivalry" suicide.

1. Sometimes objections come in pairs that are logically inconsistent with each other. This puts them in rivalry.
2. This doesn't mean that both objections are false, but it does cut your task in half, because both can't be true at the same time. Also, it may expose the potential irrationality of the person making the challenge.
3. Consider the following examples.
   a. I met a Christian man in India once who told me of a conversation he had with a Hindu who held two views inconsistent with each other.

      HINDU MAN: Is Gandhi in heaven? Heaven would be a very poor place without Gandhi in it.

      CHRISTIAN: Well, sir, you must believe in heaven, then, and apparently you have done some thinking about what would qualify someone for it. Tell me, what kind of people go to heaven? [Note his friendly tone, and his use of a variation of Columbo #1.]

      HINDU MAN: Good people go to heaven.

      CHRISTIAN: But this idea of a good person is very unclear to me. What is good? [continued use of Columbo #1]

      HINDU MAN: [*in typical Hindu fashion*] Good and bad are relative; there is no clear definition.

      CHRISTIAN: If that is true, sir, that goodness is relative and can't be defined, how is it you assume Gandhi is good and should be in heaven?

The "sibling rivalry": (a) Gandhi is good and there is an objective standard of good and evil, or (b) morality is relative and Gandhi cannot be called "good" in any ultimate sense. Since these both can't be true at the same time, there is a sibling rivalry suicide.

E. Always be alert for points of view that self-destruct.

1. Don't feel that you have to do all the work refuting a bad argument.
    a. Keep your eyes open and stay alert to see if the view commits suicide.
    b. Ask the question "Does that position carry the seeds of its own destruction?"
2. When you discover that your friend's view is self-refuting, ask a question that exploits the problem and lets him sink his own ship.

III. WHAT MAIN POINTS DID WE COVER IN THIS SESSION?

A. First, we covered the nature of self-refuting claims.

1. Suicidal views express contradictory concepts.
2. Suicidal views are necessarily false; they can't be true in any possible world.

B. Second, you learned how to recognize when someone's view self-destructs.

1. First, pay attention to the basic premise, conviction, or claim.
2. Then determine if the claim undermines itself.
    a. Does the statement satisfy its own requirements?
    b. Does it possess an internal contradiction?

C. Third, we examined the following examples of popular ideas that commit suicide and learned how to respond to them.

1. "It's wrong to try to change other people's religious beliefs."
2. "All religions are equally true and valid."
3. "You can only know what has been proven by science."
4. "There is no truth."

D. Finally, we learned how to recognize "sibling rivalry" suicide.

1. This kind of suicide happens with logically inconsistent pairs of objections that oppose each other.
2. We can eliminate at least one of the objections by pointing out the conflict.

E. In the next session, we'll talk about "taking the roof off," a powerful tactic that demonstrates how certain views are completely untenable.

INTERACTIVE STUDY

Self-Assessment

Try to answer the following questions without using your notes.

1. The Suicide tactic makes capital of the tendency of many points of view to ______________________ when given the opportunity.

2. Views that commit suicide express ________________ concepts.

3. Statements that commit suicide are also known as ________________ statements.

4. List the two steps we take to recognize a point that commits suicide.
   - First, pay attention to the basic _________, _________, or _________.
   - Second, determine if the claim satisfies its own ________________. Is there an internal _________?

5. In sibling rivalry suicide, a pair of objections are logically ________________ with each other, thus ________________ at least one.

Self-Assessment with Answers

1. The Suicide tactic makes capital of the tendency of many points of view to *self-destruct* when given the opportunity.

2. Views that commit suicide express *contradictory* concepts.

3. Statements that commit suicide are also known as *self-refuting* statements.

4. List the two steps we take to recognize a point that commits suicide.
    - First, pay attention to the basic *premise*, *conviction*, or *claim*.
    - Second, look to see if the claim satisfies its own *requirements*. Is there an internal *contradiction*?

5. In sibling rivalry suicide, a pair of objections are logically *inconsistent* with each other, thus *canceling out* at least one.

GOING DEEPER: Information for Self-Study

1. This week, work on your ambassador skills by using the Suicide tactic. See if you can discover self-refuting statements in things you read, statements you hear, or conversations you have with others.

2. Take a few friends aside and introduce them to the Suicide tactic. Describe how it works and give them a few examples.

3. Review the self-assessment exercise above so you'll be able to answer all the questions without the prompts.

FOOD FOR THOUGHT

Mass "Suicide"

Condemning Condemnation

The following dialogue was taken from a call on my radio show, and demonstrates the self-refuting nature of the claim, "It's wrong to condemn anyone for anything."

LEE: I'm not a homosexual, but I think that it's wrong to condemn anybody for anything.

GREG: Why are you condemning me, then? [Suicide tactic]

LEE: What?

GREG: I said, why are you condemning me if you think it's wrong?

LEE: I'm telling you because a lot of Christians condemn people.

GREG: Well, you're condemning me because I just condemned homosexuals as wrong.

LEE: Yes, I am. You are supposed to love everybody.

GREG: Wait a minute, you just said it's wrong to condemn people, and now you are condemning me. So I'm asking, why are you doing the same thing that you say is wrong when I do it? [narrating the argument]

LEE: No, I'm not. [*Then the light begins to dawn.*] Okay, let's put it this way. I'm not condemning you; I'm reprimanding you. Is that better?

GREG: Then my comments about homosexuals are simple reprimands as well.[21]

You Are What You Eat?

I once saw a sign in a restaurant that read, "You are what you eat." I pointed out to the waitress that this was true only if we are nothing more than our bodies. Further, if we are what we eat, we can't be anything until we have eaten something. But we can't eat something until we are something. Therefore, it can't be true that we are what we eat.

The waitress looked at me and said, "You'll have to talk to the manager."

To Err Is Human

A common attack on the Bible goes like this: Man wrote the Bible. Man is imperfect. Therefore, the Bible is imperfect and not inspired by God.

This attempt fails for two reasons. First, the conclusion doesn't logically follow because the first premise subtly presumes what it's trying to prove—that the Bible isn't inspired by God. What's at issue is whether natural man is solely responsible for the Bible or whether God worked through men and inspired the text. Since the first premise presumes the conclusion, the approach is circular.

Second, the argument commits suicide because it presumes that if man is capable of error, he will always err—that he couldn't have been involved in any sound or accurate enterprise, like writing the Bible. But if that were true, this argument itself would have to be false, because it, too, comes from an errant human. Taken at face value, this objection is self-refuting.

It doesn't follow that if man is capable of error, he always will err. It is not enough to dismiss the Bible simply by noting that "man wrote it." This, in itself, proves nothing.

Theistic Evolution Designed by Chance?

The neo-Darwinian synthesis entails a particular mechanism that *determines*—this is an important word—which changes are reproduced in the next generation. This mechanism is called "natural selection."

In natural selection, specific circumstances in the environment allow a particular individual to survive and reproduce, passing its mutated genes on to the next generation. Chance conditions in nature make the "choice," not God. If nature is selecting, then God is not selecting. The two are at odds with each other.

Either God designs the details, or nature shuffles the deck and natural selection chooses the winning hand. The mechanism is either conscious and intentional (design), or unconscious and unintentional (natural selection). Creation is teleological; it has a purpose, a goal, an end. Evolution is accidental, like a straight flush dealt to a poker rookie.

Theistic evolution, then, is belief in design by chance. That's like a square circle—there is no such thing. Blending evolution with creation is like putting a square peg in a round hole. It just doesn't fit.[22]

Freedom, Rationality, and Knowledge

Some hold that everything in life is determined by prior physical conditions and there is therefore no free will. This would also be the case if there is no soul. If there is no first-person center of our existence that exercises free will, then all of our "choices" are merely inevitable results of blind physical forces.

Here's the problem. Without freedom, there can be no rationality. None of us would be able to choose his beliefs based on reasons. We would hold our beliefs only because we had been predetermined to do so.

That's why it's odd when someone tries to *argue* for determinism. If determinism is true, then his conviction could not be based on reasons—the merits of the view itself—but on prior physical conditions that caused his belief. He would be "determined" to believe in determinism, while others would be "determined" to disagree.

Therefore, if there is no free will, no one could ever know it. Every one of our thoughts, dispositions, and opinions would have been predetermined instead of chosen for based on good reasons.

Still others limit the area of knowledge to those things that can be empirically tested. To them, all knowledge is based only on what we can know through our five senses. But is this a truth their physical senses have taught them? Of course not. Further, have they "sensed" all knowledge in order for them to know what all knowledge is like?

Can God Make a Rock So Big He Can't Lift It?

This is a pseudo-question. It is like asking, "Can God win an arm wrestling match against Himself?" or "If God beat Himself up, who would win?" or "Can God's power defeat His own power?"

The question is nonsense because, for one reason, it treats God as if He were two instead of one. The phrase "stronger than" can only be used when two subjects are in view, like when we say Bill is stronger than Bob or my left arm is stronger than my right arm. Since God is only one, it makes no sense to ask if He is stronger than Himself. That is why this is a pseudo-question. It proves nothing about any deficiency in God, because the question itself is incoherent.

The goal of this person's objection is to show that there are some things God can't do, thus undermining the Christian concept of an omnipotent Creator. This illustration, however, miscasts the biblical notion of omnipotence and is therefore guilty of misrepresenting our view, the straw man fallacy. The only way it could even begin to make sense is if it attempted to pit one aspect of God's ability against another—in this case, His creative ability against His ability to lift.

Omnipotence doesn't mean that God can do anything, however. The concept of omnipotence has to do with power. There are, in fact, many things God can't do. He can't make square circles. He can't create a morally free creature who couldn't choose evil. He can't instantly create a sixty-year-old man (not one that *looks* sixty, but one that *is* sixty). None of these, though, have anything to do with power. Instead, they are logically contradictory and therefore contrary to God's rational nature.

Tainted Thoughts

C. S. Lewis cited an example of self-refutation in his book of essays, *God in the Dock*. In response to the Freudian and Marxist claim that all thoughts are tainted (either psychologically or ideologically) at their source, Lewis wrote:

> If they say that all thoughts are thus tainted, then, of course, we must remind them that Freudianism and Marxism are as much systems of thought as Christian theology or philosophical idealism. The Freudian and the Marxian are in the same boat with all the rest of us, and cannot criticize us from the outside. They have sawn off the branch they are sitting on. If, on the other hand, they say that the taint need not invalidate their thinking, then neither need it invalidate ours. In which case they have saved their own branch, but also saved ours along with it.[23]

SESSION 5

The Taking-the-Roof-Off Tactic

Being able to give clear answers to these questions demonstrates your mastery of the information from the last session. Use this self-assessment exercise as a review of what you learned last time.

INTERACTIVE STUDY

Demonstrating Mastery

Try recalling the answers to the following questions without using your notes. The answers are located at the end of session 4.

1. Describe the Suicide tactic and why it works.

2. List the two steps to recognizing when a point commits suicide.

3. Describe sibling rivalry suicide.

INTERACTIVE STUDY

Find someone to share your experience with from last session's assignment. Did you discover any self-refuting statements in the things you read or heard, or in the conversations you had with others?

I. REVIEW

A. In the last session, we covered the following:

1. First, we learned the nature of self-refuting claims.
    a. Suicidal views express contradictory concepts.
    b. Suicidal views are necessarily false; they can't be true in any possible world.
2. Second, we learned how to recognize when someone else's view self-destructs.
    a. First, we pay attention to the basic premise, conviction, or claim.
    b. Then we determine if the claim undermines itself. We ask, "Does the statement satisfy its own requirements?" Does it have any internal contradictions?
3. Third, we examined the following examples of popular ideas that commit suicide and learned how to respond to them.
    a. "It's wrong to try to change other people's religious beliefs."
    b. "All religions are equally true and valid."
    c. "You can only know what's been proven by science."
    d. "There is no truth."
4. Finally, we learned how to recognize sibling rivalry suicide.
    a. This kind of suicide happens when pairs of objections are logically inconsistent with each other.
    b. We can eliminate at least one of the objections by pointing out the conflict.

B. In this session, you'll learn the Taking-the-Roof-Off tactic.

1. You'll see how some points of view logically lead to unacceptable conclusions.
2. You'll learn how to recognize those views and how to reduce them to their absurd consequences (*reductio ad absurdum*).
3. You'll see how man made in God's image makes this tactic possible.
4. Finally, we'll look at some specific examples of popular ideas that will lead you over a cliff if you follow them, and then I'll show you how to "take the roof off" with them.

II. THE TAKING-THE-ROOF-OFF TACTIC

A. The Taking-the-Roof-Off tactic is a simple technique used with great skill by Francis Schaeffer.

1. Consider the tactic in brief.
   a. First, you adopt the other person's viewpoint for the sake of argument.
   b. Next, you press him to the logical—and absurd—consequences of his view.
2. This tactic is also known as *reductio ad absurdum* (or simply *reductio*): reducing the argument to its absurd conclusion or consequence.

REFLECT FOR A MOMENT

The point of this tactic is to see if a person can really live in the kind of world he is affirming. Can he live with the moral or intellectual consequences of his beliefs? In essence, you're taking his moral or intellectual rules seriously and applying them consistently to show they are inadequate or absurd. The Taking-the-Roof-Off tactic makes it clear that certain arguments prove too much. The goal here is to show that one has to pay too high a price to hold certain views.

B. Here's how to take the roof off someone's argument step-by-step:

1. First, reduce the point of view to its basic premise, assertion, principle, or moral rule.
2. Second, give the idea a "test drive" and see where it goes by asking . . .
   a. If I follow this principle consistently, what would be the result?
   b. Do any absurd consequences result when this view is consistently applied?
   c. Does the rule have other unintended consequences that seem counterintuitive?
3. Third, invite the person to think about the implications of his view if it were really true.

REFLECT FOR A MOMENT

Here is why this tactic is so effective. As a point of fact, humans are made in the image of God and must live in the world God created. Consequently, every person who is a nontheist must live with a contradiction between what he says he believes and what is actually true.

In a very real sense, every person who denies God is living on borrowed capital. He enjoys living as if the world is filled with morality, meaning, order, and beauty, yet he denies the existence of the God who grounds these things and makes them possible.

Because of this, non-Christians live in a contradictory world that creates a point of tension between what they say they believe and what is actually true. Humans have erected as a defense a subconscious self-deception—a "roof," so to speak—to protect them from considering the consequences of their beliefs. Your goal is to remove that roof, expose the fraud, and deprive them of their false sense of security.

In Francis Schaeffer's words:

> Every man has built a roof over his head to shield himself at the point of tension. . . . The Christian, lovingly, must remove the shelter [the roof] and allow the truth of the external world and of what man is, to beat upon him. When the roof is off, each man must stand naked and wounded before the truth of what is. . . . He must come to know that his roof is a false protection from the storm of what is.[24]

When you find the place where that tension exists, exploit it gently, but directly. This is where a well-placed question (Columbo #3) can be really effective. Your goal is to cause the non-Christian a little pain, push him off balance, and direct him toward the logic—actually, the illogic—of his espoused beliefs.

AMBASSADOR SKILLS

To press a person's view to its logical (and absurd) conclusion, you must first understand the view. Use your Columbo tactic to probe for the details until you have a good grasp of the person's point. Then you will be in the best position to assess it and, if possible, refute it.

REFLECT FOR A MOMENT

Everyone who rejects Christianity must believe something in its place. There is no philosophical neutral ground on this issue. Even the person who refuses to decide must defend her agnosticism. If she rejects Christianity in favor of some other belief (e.g., skepticism), this leaves her open to the golden rule of apologetics: "Ask of others as they ask of you." In other words, why is her belief (or nonbelief) more reasonable than belief in Christianity?

GOING DEEPER: Information for Self-Study

Jesus also used the Taking-the-Roof-Off tactic in His interactions with the Pharisees. Notice how He reduced the Pharisees' reasoning to its logical and absurd conclusion in this encounter:

> Then they brought him a demon-possessed man who was blind and mute, and Jesus healed him, so that he could both talk and see. All the people were astonished and said, "Could this be the Son of David?"
>
> But when the Pharisees heard this, they said, "It is only by Beelzebul, the prince of demons, that this fellow drives out demons."
>
> Jesus knew their thoughts and said to them, "Every kingdom divided against itself will be ruined, and every city or household divided against itself will not stand. If Satan drives out Satan, he is divided against himself. How then can his kingdom stand?" (Matt. 12:22–26 NIV)

III. EXAMPLES OF TAKING THE ROOF OFF

Let's put into practice our three steps to taking the roof off:

A. First, consider the primary way people argue in favor of homosexuality.

1. People often justify homosexuality by claiming they were born with the "natural" tendency for it.
   a. They take this claim as a moral justification for their behavior.
   b. It doesn't follow, though, that a natural urge for something means that it's okay to fulfill that urge.
   c. It could be argued, using this line of reasoning, that if I have a "natural" tendency to beat up homosexuals, then gay bashing should be morally acceptable.
   d. Here's how it might look:

      MAN: I was born that way.

      CHRISTIAN: Let me ask you a question. What if I were born with the "natural" impulse to beat up homosexuals? Would that make gay bashing morally acceptable?

2. Clearly, appealing to alleged "natural tendencies" is not adequate to show that someone's behavior is okay.
   a. This confuses what *is* with what *ought to be*—the is/ought fallacy (aka the "naturalistic fallacy").
   b. The point of morality is to curb natural impulses that are wrong.
   c. Animals always do what comes naturally. That is not the rule for humans.
   d. The difference between "doing what comes naturally" and principled self-restraint is called "civilization."

      The basic premise: Any "natural" tendency or behavior is morally acceptable.

The reductio: If gay bashing is "natural" for me, then it is okay.

The truth: Just because it is natural doesn't mean it is moral.

B. Next, let's look at the "minimalist ethic."

1. The minimalist ethic says that any behavior is okay as long as we're not hurting anyone.
2. This moral system cannot survive, because it justifies Peeping Toms, sexual assault on unconscious victims, and necrophilia, to name a few.

The basic premise: Any behavior is okay as long as I'm not hurting anyone.

The reductio: Peeping Toms, sexual assault while someone is unconscious, and necrophilia all survive this test, but each is clearly immoral.

The truth: The minimalist ethic is not an adequate moral system.[25]

AMBASSADOR SKILLS

Here are some sample conversations that employ the Taking-the-Roof-Off tactic.

NON-CHRISTIAN: Morals are relative and are nothing more than personal preferences.

CHRISTIAN: If that's the case, then wouldn't it simply be a matter of personal preference to kill a hungry child rather than feed her? On your view, either choice is morally allowed, right? [Notice the use of the *reductio*.]

NON-CHRISTIAN: Sure, the unborn is alive in the sense that it's growing, but it's just part of the mother's body.

CHRISTIAN: If that's true, then it's possible the mother can have male sex organs as part of her own body (if she's carrying a boy) while she's pregnant. Does that make sense to you? [Notice again his use of the *reductio*.]

INTERACTIVE STUDY

Consider the ideas below. Can you find the absurdity that results from consistently applying these views? What is the basic premise entailed in each and what is the *reductio*? Some are more difficult than others. Don't be frustrated if the answers don't seem obvious at first. Quickly jot down the problem if you see it, then move to another.

- Moral relativism and theft
- Atheistic evolution and condemnation of genocide
- "I'm personally against abortion, but I don't believe in forcing my view on others."
- Capital punishment is wrong because Jesus would forgive.
- There is no truth; therefore we ought to tolerate other people's views.

GOING DEEPER: Information for Self-Study

Consider these responses to the challenges above.

Moral Relativism

The easiest way to answer someone who denies moral absolutes is to steal his stereo. Not really, of course, but this person would have to concede that theft is wrong, which is a concession to at least one objective moral principle, thus negating his relativism.

The basic premise: There are no objective moral obligations.
The reductio: Stealing (or any other behavior) is not objectively wrong.
The truth: There must be some moral absolutes.

Atheistic Evolution

If there is no God and we evolved by chance, there is no fundamental, qualitative difference between animals and humans. Yet we permit a farmer to divide the weak from the strong in his herd of cows, but we are horrified that Hitler would do the same to Jews. Why is the first right, but the second wrong given our starting point? The logical conclusion is that if God doesn't exist, there is no ultimate justification for objective ethical obligations.

The basic premise: We are governed only by the natural process of evolution.

The reductio: The strong are permitted to oppress the weak.

The truth: Evolution is not an adequate explanation for morality. God must exist to ground obvious ethical duties.

The "Modified Pro-choice" Abortion Stance

The modified pro-choice position is a politician's favorite. In the same breath, she will admit her own personal belief that abortion is wrong, but then say that others should have legal access to abortion. If she really believes that abortion actually kills an innocent human being, though, why would she want abortion to be legal for anyone?

The basic premise: Abortion should be legal, even though the politician personally believes it kills an innocent baby.

The reductio: Mothers should be allowed to kill their children, even if some of us disapprove.

The truth: The modified pro-choice position is barbaric. What kind of person champions the right to kill what she actually believes is an innocent human child?

The reductio here is easily combined with the Columbo tactic. Ask, "Why do you personally think abortion is wrong?" When she says, "Because I believe abortion takes the life of an innocent human baby," say, "Let me see if I understand you. You actually believe abortion kills an innocent human child, but you think it should be legal for mothers to do that to their children. Did I get that right?"

Capital Punishment

Mother Teresa once appealed to the governor of California to stay the execution of a murderer on the grounds that "Jesus would forgive." When applied consistently, this view disqualifies any punishment because Jesus would always forgive. While true—Jesus would forgive a person, if he repented—emptying the prisons doesn't seem to be what Jesus had in mind with forgiveness. Scripture affirms the government's authority to levy punishments for wrongdoing.[26]

The basic premise: If Jesus would forgive, then we have no right to execute murderers.

The reductio: Then no punishment of *any* kind would be justified.

The truth: The fact that Jesus would forgive does not mean that governments should not punish.

The Claim That There Is No Truth

To the person who claims there is no truth, we could say, "Then what's the point?" If there is no truth, there's no reason to continue educating ourselves. And if there is no truth, then there's no moral truth, either, and we're therefore under no obligation to tolerate people who differ from us.

The basic premise: There is no truth.

The reductio: There is no reason to go to college. There is no obligation to be tolerant of those who disagree.

The truth: If we have an obligation to be tolerant, then objective truth must exist.

The Value of Cheating

An educational philosophy called "values clarification" says that morality is an individual matter, and that each student should clarify his own values. But this view also leads to an absurd conclusion, as the following story by philosopher Christina Hoff Sommers shows:

> One of my favorite anecdotes concerns a teacher in Newton, Massachusetts, who had attended numerous values clarification workshops and was assiduously applying its techniques in her class. The day came when her class of sixth graders announced that they valued cheating and wanted to be free to do it on their tests. The teacher was very uncomfortable. Her solution? She told the children that since it was her class and since she was opposed to cheating, they were not free to cheat. "In my class you must be honest, for I value honesty. In other areas of your life you may be free to cheat."[27]

At best, the teacher has offered contradictory advice. If the *teacher* values honesty, then those are *her own* values that apply only to herself, not her students. In light of what she's just been teaching, she has no grounds to stop her students from cheating if that's the value they decide to adopt.

The Polarity of Good and Evil

Someone who claims good and evil exist in polarity—that evil must exist to balance out good—has no right to complain about suffering in certain parts of the world. If good and evil must balance out each other, then evil must exist in some places so that good can thrive in others. If this concept is reduced to its absurd conclusion, the suffering children in India must continue to suffer so that children in America can be happy.

The basic premise: Evil and good exist in a polarity, balancing out each other.

The reductio: Children must suffer in India to maintain a balance with the children in America who are happy.

The truth: It is not true that evil and good must coexist so they can balance out each other.

That's Taking the Roof Off—moving a person to the logical, and absurd, conclusion of what he believes. As Francis Schaeffer wrote, "We confront men with reality; we remove their protection and their escapes; we allow the avalanches to fall."[28]

IV. WHAT MAIN POINTS DID WE COVER IN THIS SESSION?

A. We learned the Taking-the-Roof-Off tactic.

1. First, we adopt the other person's viewpoint for the sake of argument.
2. Next, we press him to the logical—and absurd—consequences of his view.

B. We learned three steps to employ the Taking-the-Roof-Off tactic.

1. First, we reduce the point of view to its basic premise.
2. Second, we give the idea a "test drive" to determine whether any absurd consequences result when this view is consistently applied.

3. Third, we invite the person to consider the implications of his view and the truth that follows from the *reductio.*

C. We learned why this tactic works.

1. Humans are made in the image of God and must live in the world God created.
2. Every person who denies this fact lives in a contradiction that creates a point of tension.
3. To protect themselves from the tension, humans have erected a self-deception—a "roof"—to shield themselves from the logical implications of their beliefs.
4. We try to remove that roof to deprive them of their false sense of security.

D. Finally, we learned a number of ways to apply this tactic to specific challenges.

E. In our next session I'll teach you the last tactic in our series, an important defensive tactic I call Steamroller.

INTERACTIVE STUDY

Self-Assessment

Try to answer the following questions without using your notes.

1. Briefly describe the Taking-the-Roof-Off tactic.
   - First you ________ the other person's ________ for the sake of argument.
   - Next, you press him to the ________—and ________—consequences of his view.

2. Another name for this tactic, in Latin, is ________________________.

3. List the three steps of employing this tactic.
   - First, reduce the point of view to its basic _______________.
   - Second, give the idea a "test drive" to determine if any absurd ________ result from the consistent application of this view.
   - Third, invite the person to consider the ________________ of this view and the ________________ that follows from the *reductio*.

4. Explain why this tactic works.
   - Humans are made in the ________ and must live in the world that ________.
   - Every person who denies this lives in a ________ that creates a ________.
   - To protect themselves, people have erected a self-deception, or a "________," to shield themselves from the logical implications of their beliefs.
   - We try to remove that roof, depriving them of their false ________ of ________.

Self-Assessment with Answers

1. Briefly describe the Taking-the-Roof-Off tactic.
   - First you *adopt* the other person's *viewpoint* for the sake of argument.
   - Next, you press him to the *logical*—and *absurd*—consequences of his view.

2. Another name for this tactic, in Latin, is *reductio ad absurdum.*

3. List the three steps of employing this tactic.
   - First, reduce the point of view to its basic *premise.*
   - Second, give the idea a *"test drive"* to determine if any absurd *consequences* result from the consistent application of this view.
   - Third, invite the person to consider the *implications* of this view and the *truth* that follows from the *reductio.*

4. Explain why this tactic works.
   - Humans are made in the *image of God* and must live in the world that *God created.*
   - Every person who denies this lives in a *contradiction* that creates a *point of tension.*
   - To protect themselves, people have erected a self-deception—a *"roof"*—to shield them from the logical implications of their beliefs.
   - We try to remove that roof, depriving them of their false *sense* of *security.*

GOING DEEPER: Information for Self-Study

1. Be alert this week to points of view that might lead to absurd conclusions if they're practiced consistently.

2. You might want to start with the reasons people give to justify abortion.

3. Be prepared to share them with the group (if you're using this as a group study) or, if you're studying on your own, with a friend who you're helping learn the tactical approach.

FOOD FOR THOUGHT

Unfortunately, most people hold to beliefs they haven't considered carefully and that often lead to absurd consequences. The following vignettes tackle a number of those views by employing the Taking-the-Roof-Off tactic. Notice the variety of ways this tactic can be used.

The Problem of Evil

The dialogue below employs three tactics—the Columbo tactic, the Suicide tactic, and the Taking-the-Roof-Off tactic—and concerns the problem of evil. Many people reject a belief in God because of the evil they see in the world. If you're a relativist, though, this objection commits suicide. As it turns out, the presence of evil in the world is one of the best evidences for God, not against Him.

CHRISTIAN: You said earlier that you don't believe in God or any moral absolutes. Now you're asking me how God can exist when there is so much evil in the world. Is that right? [Columbo #1]

NONBELIEVER: That's right.

CHRISTIAN: So you do believe in evil?

NONBELIEVER: Of course. That's the reason for my objection.

CHRISTIAN: This may sound like a silly question, but what is this evil you're talking about? Can you define it for me? [Again, note the use of the first Columbo question, "What do you mean by that?"]

NONBELIEVER: You know, famines, earthquakes, murders, disease, rape, pillaging—that kind of thing.

CHRISTIAN: So you're concerned about human evil and natural evil, right?

NONBELIEVER: Something like that, yes.

CHRISTIAN: You mentioned earthquakes, disease, famine . . . all of which are natural evils. Aren't you an evolutionist?

NONBELIEVER: Of course! You don't think I'm a creationist, do you?

CHRISTIAN: No, of course not. But that raises a question for me. Why is a "natural" thing like a tidal wave or an earthquake evil? You wouldn't call a two-foot shore break evil, would you?

NONBELIEVER: No, but tidal waves and earthquakes cause damage; people get killed.

CHRISTIAN: So what? Should that matter? [This begins the Taking-the-Roof-Off tactic.] Living things die every day, making food for other living things. That's the balance of nature, isn't it? It is the beautiful thing about "Mother Nature." Any city wiped out by the tidal wave becomes food for crabs and starfish who are better adapted to survive underwater and eat the refuse that comes their way. From the crabs' perspective, tidal waves are great. The same thing happens when someone gets AIDS. So what's your complaint?

It seems to me that from an evolutionary perspective, one organism beats up on another in its struggle to survive. One man's funeral is another worm's smorgasbord. What's wrong with that? We try to kill the virus; the virus tries to kill us. No judgments. It is all part of the dance. You'd probably call killing a typhoid germ good, but if it kills you, that's bad. Isn't that kind of a self-centered view of natural evil where humans are concerned?

NONBELIEVER: But I don't want to die!

CHRISTIAN: Neither do I, but now we're talking about our personal desires, not the moral problem of earthquakes and disease.

NONBELIEVER: You aren't suggesting a germ and a human being have the same value?

CHRISTIAN: Oh, I'm not suggesting it at all. I don't believe they do. But I have a reason why I don't believe that, a justification for viewing bugs one way and human beings another. What I'm trying to figure out is how you could possibly believe that a human death is ultimately more "evil" than the death of a virus if evolution is true and chance rules the universe. [Again, this is an extension of the Taking-the-Roof-Off tactic.] Any suggestions? Can you clear this up for me? [Note a movement back to Columbo #3.]

NONBELIEVER: I don't get it.

CHRISTIAN: My question is simple. If we live in a chance universe of blind cause-and-effect where no God exists, how can you refer to some accidents of nature as evil—not just unpleasant or disliked, but evil? That's a moral judgment, isn't it? Is nature immoral? [Again, note the use of Columbo #3.]

NONBELIEVER: I don't know how to explain it.

CHRISTIAN: Well, maybe we can do better with human evil.

NONBELIEVER: Right, Hitler and drive-by killings and stuff. How can your God allow that?

CHRISTIAN: I need to ask you another question just for my clarification. You're saying those things like genocide and drive-by shootings are evil? [Columbo #1]

NONBELIEVER: Of course they are!

CHRISTIAN: What I'm trying to understand is this: Is that only your opinion, or does your moral view apply to everyone else? [Request for further clarification]

NONBELIEVER: That's evil to me. That's my truth.

CHRISTIAN: So, ultimately, those things are only evil from your perspective?

NONBELIEVER: That's my opinion.

CHRISTIAN: Okay, I accept that. But if that's so, I don't really understand your objection. If I have it right, your objection to God goes something like this: "I don't believe in God because there's evil in the world, and evil is whatever I define it to be." It sounds to me like you won't believe in God because some things happen that you don't like, but those things might be okay for others. You don't like killing (that's your moral truth), but others might think it's fine. Nazis had no problem killing Jews, for example. So, there's no right or wrong here, only different feelings about it. [Taking the Roof Off again]

NONBELIEVER: No! I think what the Nazis did was terrible.

CHRISTIAN: You mean it was truly wrong, immoral in some objective sense, regardless of who did it and when they did it?

NONBELIEVER: To me, it was wrong. In my opinion, that was evil.

CHRISTIAN: See, this is what confuses me about your question. You say that what the Nazis did was evil, and you're asking why God allows that kind of evil. Then you say that evil is only a matter of opinion. So it sounds like you're asking, "Why does God allow something that's against my opinion?"

Let me put my question another way. It sounds to me like you're saying, "I can't believe in God because stewed cabbage exists." I say, "What's wrong with stewed cabbage?" You say, "I hate the stuff." The fact is, I personally agree with you about stewed cabbage, but some people think it's great. However, just because you don't like stewed cabbage doesn't mean God can't exist. So I'm asking, how can you say God can't exist just because you didn't happen to like the Nazis? A lot of people loved them. [Again, the third use of Columbo]

It seems to me that your objection says more about your personal tastes than it does about God's existence. What am I missing here?

NONBELIEVER: But murder and vegetables are two different things!

CHRISTIAN: How so?

NONBELIEVER: Come on. It's self-evident.

CHRISTIAN: I agree entirely, and that's my concern. [Notice that until now, the Christian hasn't argued any point yet. He has simply questioned the nonbeliever's position.]

I hold that there are objective moral principles, not laws that we make, but laws that are outside of mere personal opinion. For example, say I made up a law that all property within a twenty-mile radius of my house belonged to me and you lived fifteen miles away. I could pass out fliers announcing that everyone on "my" property has to move. Would you move? No, because I have no authority. But if the state decided to put a freeway through your backyard, you'd begin looking for a new place to live because the state is a legitimate authority for that kind of thing. It seems to me that there can only be a binding moral principle ("It's wrong to murder or steal") if a legitimate authority is involved.

In the same way, evil—real evil, the kind that creates these dilemmas for us—must be defined by some objective standard outside of us before we can really beef about it. And the minute we have agreed to that, we have to acknowledge that there must be a legitimate authority outside of our own feelings (God?) that makes sense of the existence of evil before we can complain about it. Ironically, the kind of human evil you're talking about—oppression, murder, violence—only happens when specific moral absolutes are rejected and men begin treating other men like mere animals. That invariably happens whenever men or governments contend there is no God to whom we must answer.

Abortion for Rape Victims?

If we allowed an abortion in the case of rape, it would send a terrible message. That message would be that when someone reminds you of something extremely painful, you could eliminate them. But you can't kill another human being just because their existence makes your life physically or emotionally burdensome.

Trotting Out the Toddler[29]

Virtually every argument for abortion could equally justify killing newborns. If it's wrong to take the life of innocent human beings on one side of the birth canal, it seems wrong to take their lives on the other. Conversely, if abortion is justifiable, then euthanasia would be acceptable for the same reasons. A seven-inch journey down the birth canal cannot miraculously transform a nonhuman tissue mass into a valuable human being we should shelter and protect.

That's why when discussing abortion we use a version of Taking the Roof Off called "Trotting Out the Toddler." We can say, "Do you realize that the principle you're advancing not only takes away the rights of a fetus, but also of a newborn? Wouldn't newborns also be in danger if, for example, something like self-awareness is what makes humans valuable? Newborns aren't self-aware."

When someone says, "Women have the right to choose," respond by trotting out the toddler again. That is, ask if the reason they give for abortion is an adequate reason to kill a toddler.[30] Ask, "Should a woman have the right to choose to kill her two-year-old child?" Since both the unborn and the toddler are human beings, the same moral rule should apply to each. One way out is to argue that the unborn is not a true human being, but this is scientifically unsound.

Sometimes when you use this tactic, the other person will respond, "I never thought about that." And that's the point. People don't think their ideas out to the logical conclusions. It is our job to help them see their mistakes.

Were You Ever an Unborn Child?

It doesn't seem to make sense to refer to yourself as a former sperm or egg. Does it make sense, though, to talk about yourself before you were born? Did you turn in your mother's womb or kick when you were startled by a loud noise? Did you suck your thumb? Were those your experiences or someone else's?

If you were once the unborn child your mother carried, then you must accept an undeniable truth: Killing that child through abortion would have killed you. Not a potential you. Not a possible you. Not a future you. Abortion would have killed *you.*

This is why abortion is tragic: It kills more than a human body. It kills a valuable human being.

Caring for the Kids

A standard objection to the pro-life view is that pro-lifers have no right to oppose abortion unless they're willing to care for the woman and her child. If you're confronted with this challenge, take a moment to restate the claim without the spin. What's actually being asserted is amazing, when you think about it.

"If I understand you right," you might say, "you're saying I can't object to killing unborn children unless I'm willing to care for those children. Is that right?" Then ask, "Do you really believe that I can only object to killing children if I'm willing to raise them myself? Why would you believe a thing like that?"

It simply does not follow that because one objects to the killing of innocent human beings, he must be willing to care for those who survive. Imagine, for example, how bizarre it would sound if someone argued, "You have no right telling me not to beat my wife unless you're willing to marry her" or "Unless you are willing to hire ex-slaves for your business, you have no right to oppose slavery." (Indeed, slave owners used this very argument 150 years ago.) In the same way, abortion is not justified if pro-lifers fail to care for those (both mother and baby) involved in a crisis pregnancy.

As a point of fact, though, there are hundreds of pregnancy centers all over the country run and funded by pro-lifers who are willing to care for those mothers involved in crisis pregnancies—pro-life service providers dedicated to the well-being of mothers who choose life for their children. They provide medical aid, pregnancy support, housing, baby clothing, cribs, food, adoption services—even post-abortion counseling services—and all at no cost.

"Unnatural" Adoption

The line of reasoning that justifies homosexuality because it's a "natural" desire for those born that way annihilates the argument for adoption rights by homosexuals. If homosexuality is right because it's natural, then adoption by homosexuals must be wrong because it's unnatural. If nature dictates morality, and the natural consequence for homosexuals is to be childless, then it's unnatural—and therefore immoral—for homosexuals to raise children. Artificial insemination of lesbians or adoptions by homosexual couples would be wrong by their own reasoning. The same principle governs both issues.

Climate Control

A chorus of voices charges that Christians, through their moralizing about homosexuality, are promoting a climate of hate. The phrase of choice is "less than." By claiming homosexuality is evil, Christians demote homosexuals to a "less than" status. If a homosexual is labeled "less than," he becomes the object of scorn, hatred, and physical abuse, they say.

This is twisted logic. This kind of thinking would make Alcoholics Anonymous responsible every time a drunk gets beat up in an alley. It simply does not follow that moral condemnation of homosexuality encourages gay bashing.

Such a tactic is equally dangerous to those who use it. According to them, taking a moral position is called "hate." But their own objection to hate is also a moral position. Are those who demonize Christians for their views equally guilty of hatemongering? Clearly this kind of attack is not really about principle, but about politically correct viewpoints.

Life a Beautiful Choice?

Believe it or not, a pastor once said, "'Life a beautiful choice'? It's not so beautiful for an unwanted child." I had to ask myself, "Why can't an unwanted child's life be beautiful?" Presumably, the answer is, "Because he's unwanted." But this alone doesn't make anyone's life miserable. There's more to it than this. What makes an unwanted child's life miserable? Other people do. Unwanted children are unhappy because they're treated as unwanted.

This pastor's startling admission amounts to this: "If we let this child live, we're going to treat him so badly and will make life so miserable for him that he'll wish he were dead." It's an admission that it's better to kill a child than do what's necessary to give that child a meaningful life. And the pastor seemed to think this was a good argument for abortion.

Morality from Nature?

It is common of late to justify one's "sexual orientation" by an appeal to nature. The claim "I was born this way" is all that is needed to stem moral criticism of homosexuality. But why settle for this approach? Why think that the state of nature is an appropriate guide to morality?

Seventeenth-century philosopher Thomas Hobbes noted famously, "Life in an unregulated state of nature is solitary, poor, nasty, brutish, and short." It was precisely this fact, according to Hobbes, that caused humans to enter into social contracts, gladly accepting the moral constraints of civilization to its alternative, the law of nature. Morality, as an extension of that contract, is a way of protecting ourselves from the brutality of living in a world where people simply did what came naturally.

Since living according to nature would justify all kinds of barbarism, how does it make sense to invoke the natural state of things to justify anything morally? Behavior that is "natural" is the very thing morality is meant to protect us from. Morality that counters one's natural inclinations rather than approves of them is our only refuge from a life that is "solitary, poor, nasty, brutish, and short."

Earth Day for Evolutionists?

Has anyone else but me noticed an inherent contradiction in the underlying convictions that drive annual Earth Day celebrations? The vast majority of those who attend such fetes are Darwinists who believe humans have a moral obligation to protect the environment. But why?

For millions of years, Mother Nature has spewed noxious fumes and poisonous gasses into the atmosphere and littered the landscape with ash and lava. Indeed, the most "natural" condition in the universe is death. As far as we know, life on Earth is completely unique; death reigns everywhere else.

Species have passed into extinction at a steady rate from the beginning of time, the strong supplanting the weak. Why shouldn't they? Each is in a struggle to the death for survival. It is a dance of destruction that fuels the evolutionary process as each creature seeks to exploit every other for its own benefit. That's evolution.

No locust swarm stops short of denuding a field because it ought to "leave a bit for the crickets. After all, we all have a right to be here." The logic of naturalism and the rules of evolution allow humans to use the environment any way we want to satisfy our own needs, just like everything else does.

The moral obligations underpinning Earth Week activities simply do not follow from the naturalistic, Darwinist worldview. Human obligation makes sense only in a theistic worldview in which God has created humans as unique and given them responsibility over the Earth to care for it. Earth Week makes sense for Christians, not Darwinists.

Christian "Faith" vs. Knowledge

For many Christians, faith and knowledge are diametrically opposed. The more evidence you have, they claim, the less faith is involved. The more bizarre and unbelievable the claim, the greater the faith needed. The greatest faith, then, would be the one farthest removed from reason or evidence.

Two odd conclusions follow from this kind of thinking.

First, apologetics—giving evidence in defense of faith—would actually be detrimental to genuine faith. Yet Peter tells us to always be ready to give an *apologia*, a defense, for the hope that is in us (1 Peter 3:15).

Second, if faith and knowledge are inversely proportional, then the more evidence we can find *against* Christianity, the better for our faith. Indeed, believing something we knew to be false would be a great virtue, biblically. God would be most pleased, on this view, with those who knew the resurrection never happened, yet still believed.

The apostle Paul called such a person pitiful, however: "If there is no resurrection of the dead, then not even Christ has been raised. And if Christ has not been raised, our preaching is useless and so is your faith. . . . And if Christ has not been raised, your faith is futile; you are still in your sins. Then those also who have fallen asleep in Christ are lost. If only for this life we have hope in Christ, we are of all people most to be pitied" (1 Cor. 15:13–14, 17–19 NIV).

According to Paul, if we believe contrary to fact, we believe in vain and are fools.

SESSION 6

The Steamroller Tactic

Being able to give clear answers to these questions demonstrates your mastery of the information from the last session. Use this self-assessment exercise as a review of what you learned last time.

INTERACTIVE STUDY

Demonstrating Mastery

Try recalling the answers to the following questions without using your notes. The answers are located at the end of session 5.

1. Briefly describe the Taking-the-Roof-Off tactic.

2. Another name for this tactic is ________________________.

3. List the three steps of employing this tactic.
    - First, ____.
    - Second, ____.
    - Third, ____.

4. Explain why this tactic works.

INTERACTIVE STUDY

Share with someone your results from the last session's assignment. Did you encounter any claims that led to logical—and absurd—conclusions?

I. REVIEW

A. In the last session, we covered the following:

1. You learned a tactic called "Taking the Roof Off."
   a. First, we learned to adopt the other person's viewpoint for the sake of argument.
   b. Next, we learned the value of pressing him to the logical—and absurd—consequences of his view.
2. You learned three steps used to employ the tactic.
   a. First, reduce the point of view to its basic premise.
   b. Second, give the idea a "test drive" to determine if any absurd consequences result when we consistently apply this view.
   c. Third, invite the person to consider the implications of his view and the truth that follows from the *reductio*.
3. You also learned why this tactic works.
   a. Humans are made in the image of God and must live in the world that God created.
   b. Every person who denies this lives in a contradiction that creates a point of tension.
   c. To protect themselves, humans have erected a self-deception—a "roof"—to shield themselves from the logical implications of their beliefs.
   d. We try to remove that roof to deprive them of their false sense of security.
4. Finally, you learned a number of ways to apply this tactic to specific challenges.

B. In this session, we'll cover the Steamroller tactic.

1. You'll learn how to recognize a steamroller (it's not hard).
2. You'll learn three steps to stop the steamroller and put you back in control of the conversation.

II. THE STEAMROLLER, A DEFENSIVE TACTIC

A. What is a steamroller?

1. Steamrollers are people who overwhelm you.
2. Steamrollers have strong opinions and strong personalities.
3. They keep you off balance and on the defensive by overwhelming you with a lot of attitude, and a lot of noise.
4. Their words come fast and furious, keeping you from collecting your wits and giving a thoughtful answer.

B. How do steamrollers operate?

1. Steamrollers have one defining characteristic: They interrupt constantly.
   a. They will cut you off before you can respond to their challenge.
   b. As soon as you begin to answer, steamrollers find something they don't like in your explanation, interrupt you, then pile on more challenges.
   c. Try to respond again, only to be interrupted again.
   d. The steamroller continues to fire questions, constantly interrupting—even changing the subject—overwhelming you, and never listening to anything you say.
   e. If this description sounds familiar, you have been steamrolled.
2. Steamrollers are insincere.[31]
   a. Steamrollers know it's easier to ask hard questions than to listen to hard answers.
   b. Steamrollers are usually not interested in answers, but in winning through intimidation.

INTERACTIVE STUDY

Share your experiences with steamrollers with someone. What was it like? How did it make you feel? How did you deal with it?

C. Here's how to deal with a steamroller in three steps.

1. Step #1: Stop the interruption graciously, but firmly, then negotiate an agreement.
    a. Many times all you need to do is simply hold up your hand and gently say, "I'm not quite finished yet."
    b. If necessary, ask for adequate time by saying, "Hold on a minute, I need a little more time. You asked a good question, and you deserve an answer. Are you interested in what I have to say?"
    c. If the steamroller is especially aggressive, calmly wait for a clear opening; don't try to talk over him if he's not cooperating.
    d. Basically you're asking him to give you something (patience) so that you can give him something in return (a chance to respond to his question or challenge).
    e. Look at the following examples of the first step of the Steamroller tactic.
        1) "Is it okay with you if I take a few moments to answer your concerns before you ask another question? I'll give you a chance to respond when I get done."
        2) "I know you have a lot of questions. But I need a moment to explain myself. Is that okay?"
        3) "Let me respond to your first challenge. When I'm done you can jump in again. Is that okay?"
        4) "That's a good question, and it deserves a decent answer. I need a moment to give you one. Is that okay?"
    f. Be sure to respond adequately to the first issue before you are forced to tackle another. Take one thing at a time.

g. When you've made your point, ask your friend to acknowledge your response. Ask a question like "Is that a fair answer to your question?" or "Does that sound plausible to you?"

h. Don't take unfair advantage of the time you buy in the negotiation.
   1) Make your point, then let him back into the conversation.
   2) Don't become a steamroller yourself—give the other side a fair chance to make a point or offer a reply.

INTERACTIVE STUDY

Think—Pair—Share

Find a partner to practice step #1 with. The first person should ask a simple question, such as "What political party do you support and why?" and then begin to interrupt when the second person attempts an answer. Use the first step in the Steamroller defense to regain control of the conversation.

AMBASSADOR SKILLS

Grace under Fire

When I face an aggressive challenger, I often give him the last word. Not only is this a gracious thing to do, but it's powerful, conveying a deep sense of confidence in your own view. Instead of fighting for the last word, give it away. Make your concluding point clearly and succinctly, and then say, "I'll let you have the last word." But don't break this promise—grant him his parting shot, and then let it rest.

2. Step #2: Shame the steamroller.
   a. If the steamroller breaks trust with your first agreement, or maybe you can't succeed in stopping him to briefly negotiate, you need to be more aggressive.

b. Shame him by taking the same approach you did in step #1, but be more direct in addressing bad manners.

c. Ask very explicitly for courtesy in your conversation. Make sure you are calm when you do, though. It will do you no good if you come across annoyed at this point.

d. Ignore his new challenges; don't follow the rabbit trail. Instead, address the steamroller problem directly.

   1) "I need to know if you really want an answer from me. I assume you asked the question because you wanted a response, but I could be wrong—you keep interrupting. Which is it?" (Wait for an affirmation.)

   2) "Could I ask you a favor? I'd love to respond to your concern, but I can't because you keep interrupting. Could I have a few moments to develop my point without being cut off? Then you can tell me what you think. Is that okay with you?" (Wait for a response.)

   3) "Can I ask you a quick question? I need to know whether you want an answer to your challenge, or if you just want to talk. When you keep interrupting me, I get the impression you don't really want an answer. If all you want is an audience, just let me know, and I'll listen. But if you want an answer, you'll have to give me time to respond. Which do you want? I need to know before we continue." (Wait for an answer.)

   4) "Here's what I have in mind. You ask your question or make your point, and I'll listen. When you're done, I'll respond and you won't interrupt. When I'm done, it will be my turn to be polite and let you have your say. I need to know if that's okay with you. If not, this conversation is over. What would you like to do?" (Wait for a response.)

e. Next, return to the steamroller's original challenge and deal with it: "Now, your challenge as I understand it is this . . . [repeat the question]. Here is how I'd like to respond."

f. Finally, don't be snippy or smug—stay focused, pleasant, and gracious while in control.

AMBASSADOR SKILLS

Example *d* is very aggressive. If you started this way, you would come off belligerent and rude. At some point, though, a direct approach is the only thing that will save the conversation. Remember, steamrollers are strong and aggressive, and sometimes they must be answered in kind.

3. Step #3: When all else fails, leave the steamroller.
   a. If he won't let you answer, listen politely until he's finished, then drop it.
   b. Let him have the satisfaction of having the last word, then politely end the conversation and walk away.
   c. Wisdom dictates not wasting time with this kind of person.

REFLECT FOR A MOMENT

Pearls before Swine

Jesus warns us, "Do not give dogs what is sacred; do not throw your pearls to pigs" (Matt. 7:6 NIV). How do we know when to speak and when to keep our pearls to ourselves? The answer is in the rest of the verse: "If you do, they may trample them under their feet, and turn and tear you to pieces."

We should be generous with the truth unless we encounter someone who shows utter contempt for the precious gift being offered. If the one you're talking with is the kind of person who will take what is holy, trample on it, and then turn on you, don't waste your time. There are others who will be more receptive.

III. WHAT MAIN POINTS DID WE COVER IN THIS SESSION?

A. First, we learned how to recognize a steamroller.

1. Steamrollers overpower you with their strong personalities.
2. Steamrollers interrupt constantly.

B. Second, we learned three steps to deal with a steamroller and put you back in control of the conversation.

1. Step 1: Stop him—Stop the interruption graciously but firmly, then negotiate an agreement.
2. Step 2: Shame him—Ask, in a very direct way, for courtesy.
3. Step 3: Leave him—Let him have the last word, then let it go.

INTERACTIVE STUDY

Self-Assessment

Try to answer the following questions without using your notes.

1. Steamrollers are people who ____________________ you with their ____________ ____________________.

2. The defining characteristic of a steamroller is ________________.

3. The first step in dealing with a steamroller is to ________________ graciously, but firmly, then ________________.

4. The second step in dealing with a steamroller is to ________________ by asking in a very direct way for ______________________.

5. The third step in dealing with a steamroller is to ________________. Let him have the last ________, then __________________________.

Self-Assessment with Answers

1. Steamrollers are people who *overpower* you with their *strong personalities.*

2. The defining characteristic of a steamroller is *interruption.*

3. The first step in dealing with a steamroller is to *stop the interruption* graciously, but firmly, then *negotiate an agreement.*

4. The second step in dealing with a steamroller is to *shame him* by asking in a very direct way for *courtesy.*

5. The third step in dealing with a steamroller is to *leave him.* Let him have the last *word*, then *walk away.*

GOING DEEPER: Information for Self-Study

1. If you encounter a steamroller this week, take a deep breath, then carefully begin to apply the steps described in this chapter to manage the encounter. Stay relaxed and try not to get defensive.
2. Don't be hard on yourself if the conversation doesn't go smoothly for you. Steamrollers are often tough to handle. It may take a little time for you to learn how to graciously navigate the challenge.
3. Introduce a few friends to the Steamroller tactic. Describe how it works and give them a few examples. They'll be glad to have a technique to help them manage the aggressive interruptions that are characteristic of steamrollers.
4. Review the previous self-assessment exercise so you'll be able to answer all the questions without the prompts.

FOOD FOR THOUGHT

Tactics and Common Ground

While interacting with others, I've found it helpful to try to frame my comments in the context of the other person's interests, discipline, or profession.

For example, when an attorney tells me he won't believe in the soul because it can't be measured physically, I ask him how he can prove in court that a motive exists when it cannot be measured physically, either. Even the laws that are the stock-in-trade of his profession are not physical. They can't be weighed. They have no chemical composition. They aren't located in space. The attorney must face the fact that the practice of his own profession defeats his objection against the soul (Taking the Roof Off).

This approach makes it easier to persuade him, because he sees my point in light of things he already knows to be true or procedures that he's already familiar with.

Learning to contextualize your points by tying your comments or explanations to relevant parts of the other person's world establishes common ground—and is an important tactical skill of an effective ambassador.

Teaching an Old Dog New Tricks

Very few people quickly admit that their beliefs have been wrong, so don't expect anyone to surrender too much ground right away. Changing beliefs is hard. Usually it's a slow process for someone to admit his error, especially when a lot is at stake.

So, don't try to move too quickly. Simplify an issue by breaking it into smaller parts. Take it step-by-step and piece by piece. Try to make headway on only one part at a time. Do everything you can to help your friend feel comfortable with the process. Don't bruise the fruit. Instead of forcing an issue, be confident that a sovereign God will use your efforts.

SESSION 7

The Inside Out Tactic

INTERACTIVE STUDY

Demonstrating Mastery

Try recalling the answers to the following questions without using your notes. The answers are located at the end of session 6.

1. Briefly describe the Steamroller tactic.
   - Steamrollers are people who ____________________ you with their ____________________.

2. What is the defining characteristic of a steamroller?
   - The defining characteristic of a steamroller is ________________.

3. Describe the first step used to deal with a steamroller.
   - The first step in dealing with a steamroller is to ________________ graciously, but firmly, then ________________.

4. Describe the second step used to deal with a steamroller.
   - The second step in dealing with a steamroller is to ________________ by asking in a very direct way for ________________________.

5. Describe the third step used to deal with a steamroller.
   - The third step in dealing with a steamroller is to ________________. Let him have the last ________, then ________________________.

INTERACTIVE STUDY

Find someone with whom to share your experience from last session's assignment. Did you encounter any steamrollers in the conversations you had with others? Were you able to apply the steps of the Steamroller tactic? How did it go?

I. REVIEW

A. In the last session, we covered the following:

1. You learned a tactic called "Steamroller."
   a. First, we learned that steamrollers are people who overwhelm you with their strong opinions and strong personalities.
   b. Next, we learned the defining characteristic of steamrollers is they interrupt constantly without really listening to what you have to say.
   c. Steamrollers are usually not interested in answers, but in winning through intimidation.
2. You learned three steps used to deal with a steamroller.
   a. Step #1, stop the interruption graciously, but firmly, then negotiate an agreement, asking for adequate time to respond without being interrupted.
   b. Step #2, shame the steamroller by politely, but directly, addressing the bad manners and trying a second time to negotiate a fair interaction.
   c. Step #3, when all else fails, simply discontinue the conversation and leave the steamroller.
3. You also learned that not everyone deserves an answer.

a. Jesus warns, "Do not give dogs what is sacred; do not throw your pearls to pigs" (Matt. 7:6 NIV).

b. Be generous with the truth unless you encounter someone who shows utter contempt for the precious gift being offered.

c. Wisdom dictates not wasting time with this kind of person.

B. In this session, we'll cover the Inside Out tactic.

1. You'll learn an insight—that God has built certain information inside every human being that he cannot deny—that will help you navigate creatively in a variety of circumstances.
2. You'll see how the "mannishness of man," the image of God in man, informs how people react in ways contrary to their expressed view of the world.
3. We'll look at a number of examples of how a person's mannishness betrays his false worldview.
4. You'll also learn how sometimes an appeal to a person's existential need—their deep human longing—can be more powerful than a straightforward argument.

II. THE INSIDE OUT TACTIC

A. The Inside Out tactic is not so much a specific maneuver as a frame of mind, an understanding of what it means to be a human living in God's world.

1. It provides an insight that will help you maneuver confidently—even creatively, sometimes—in your conversations with others.
2. In a sense, we have inside information on others that they will eventually acknowledge—sometimes without realizing it—if we just pay attention.

REFLECT FOR A MOMENT

One of atheism's most colorful apologists, Richard Dawkins, believes that morality is just a relativistic trick of evolution to get our selfish genes into the next generation. The universe, he says, is a place with "no design, no purpose, no evil, no good, nothing but blind, pitiless indifference."[32] That statement is completely consistent with his naturalism.

Yet at another time he rails against the God of the Old Testament as a "vindictive, bloodthirsty, homophobic, racist, genocidal, sadomasochistic, malevolent bully."[33]

Do you see the problem? This second statement is not consistent with Dawkins's naturalism. Rather it's his commonsense moral realism doing the talking, perfectly consistent with the world that actually exists—God's world.[34]

There is something true on the inside for Dawkins—something he knows—that he cannot help but display on the outside, in unguarded moments. When he's defending his philosophical turf, he tells the lie. When his guard is down, his humanity betrays him and he tells the truth in spite of himself.

B. The mannishness of man

1. The Inside Out tactic is based on an insight I learned from the late Francis Schaeffer that has helped me navigate more confidently in conversations with others about Christ.
2. Schaeffer called it the "mannishness of man." The concept is tied to this question: "What does it mean to be human?"
3. In Schaeffer's words, "Man is different from non-man."[35] Human beings are special, unique, unlike anything else in the created realm, "crowned . . . with glory and honor," as David put it in Psalm 8:5 (NIV).
4. That is the mannishness of man.

REFLECT FOR A MOMENT

Notice how naturalistic atheists answer the question, "What does it mean to be human?" According to pop "Science Guy" Bill Nye, we're just "a speck, on a speck, orbiting a speck, among other specks."[36] Carl Sagan said, "We emerged from microbes and muck. . . . We find ourselves in bottomless free fall . . . lost in a great darkness, and there's no one to send out a search party."[37]

And they are right, of course, in a world without God. Humans are nothing but cogs in the celestial machine, cosmic junk, the ultimate unplanned pregnancy. Nihilism—bleak nothing-ism. That's it. The key to the Inside Out tactic, though, is that no one really believes this, not deep inside.

C. Why the tactic works

1. The Christian worldview gives a better answer—a more accurate answer—to the question, "What does it mean to be human?"
   a. At the core of our beings lies a mark. It's an imprint of God himself—not *on* us, as if foreign and attached, but *in* us, as a natural feature built into our natures.
   b. This mark is part of what makes us what we are and who we are. We wouldn't be humans without it. We would only be creatures.
   c. Carl Sagan says we are cousins of apes.[38] That is Mother Nature's assessment. Father says different. Because of this mark, we are not kin to apes. We are kin to the God who made us for himself.
   d. And this is something we all know—believer and nonbeliever.
2. Here's the main insight of the Inside Out tactic:
   a. Because we all live in God's world and we are all made in God's image, there are things all people know that are embedded deep within their hearts, even though they deny them or their worldviews disqualify them.
   b. That which is already on the inside, put there by God himself, eventually shows itself on the outside—in actions, in language, and in convictions. Our mannishness cannot be suppressed.

REFLECT FOR A MOMENT

Paul wrote, "That which is known about God is evident within them; for God made it evident to them" (Rom. 1:19). This knowledge can make a big difference in your conversations.

3. Here is my tactical application of the mannishness of man:
   a. The profound truths we all know on the inside always eventually reveal themselves on the outside.
   b. All you need to do is listen.

INTERACTIVE STUDY

Couple up with another person and think about some of the ways the mannishness of man is unwittingly expressed by non-Christians when their guards are down, when they reflexively make statements that are inconsistent with the worldview they say they embrace, but perfectly dovetail with a biblical worldview. Have you noticed in the past where others borrowed *from* our worldview to make their point *against* our worldview? Discuss the conflict.

III. THE INSIDE OUT TACTIC IN PLAY

A. Two deaths

1. In the late days of summer 1997, two well-known and well-loved women died within days of each other, but the public reaction to each death was very different.
   a. Mother Teresa passed away peacefully at eighty-seven, her death a quiet conclusion to a noble life well lived.
   b. Princess Diana died in her prime at thirty-six, her death a tragic, "untimely" intrusion into a life filled with promise.
2. Why did so many react so differently to the same kind of event—a life ending, a human being dying?

   a. From one point of view—an atheistic, materialistic one—no one dies before their time. Death is death and arrives when it arrives.
   b. There's no timeliness for anything, since there is no timetable—no schedule, no plan of how things are supposed to be.
   c. In a godless universe, where all meaning is of our own making, what could it possibly mean to say someone died an untimely death?
3. People reacted differently for two reasons:
   a. Because they know life has ultimate purpose and deep significance that transcends private projects.
   b. In spite of their pontifications to the contrary, their mannishness gives them away.

B. Use the Inside Out tactic to get someone thinking.

1. First, listen to the way people talk.
   a. Listen for when—from their own mouths—their acknowledgment of reality intrudes on their philosophies.
   b. Listen for when their words—sometimes without their realizing it—betray their true convictions about the world.
2. Second, exploit that tension by asking a question.
   a. In a world without purpose, why is Princess Di's death a tragedy?
   b. If there is no ultimate, universal morality, how can anything be really evil?
   c. Why try to talk someone out of a suicide? If there is no meaning to life, what's the point?

REFLECT FOR A MOMENT

Mother Teresa finished her course; Princess Diana did not. That is the victory and the tragedy of those events in the final days of summer 1997. But only because there is a divinely intended purpose—a noble end humans have been designed for that sin, sadly, disrupts.

IV. THE WORLD IS BROKEN AND WE ARE BROKEN

A. Everyone knows something has gone terribly wrong with the world.

1. We call it the problem of evil.
2. It prompts the question, "Why is there so much badness in the world?"

B. We all know that we are broken too.

1. Though humans have inherent dignity, we are also cruel. The evil is "out there," as it were, but it is also "in here"—in us.
   a. We are not machines that are malfunctioning.
   b. We are not bodies that are ailing.
   c. We are subjects who revolted, rebels who are now morally corrupted.
2. Again, each of us knows this deep down inside. We are the "others" doing those evil deeds we object to.

C. We are guilty, and for this we must answer.

1. Deep inside us is a gnawing awareness of our own badness, producing a feeling we universally recognize. It's called guilt. We owe.
2. We are in debt, not to a standard, not to a rule, not to a law, but to a Person—to the One we have offended with our disobedience.
3. This is not good news, because our guilt has severe consequences.

V. JUSTICE OR MERCY

A. Justice

1. Everyone longs for justice.
2. We speak of it often, especially when we've suffered injustice.
3. That's the inside revealing itself on the outside again.

4. Justice is not satisfied in this life, though. It is satisfied in the next.
   a. In Revelation 20 we find a dark passage telling of the final event of history as we know it.
   b. There's a great trial on a great plain where the guilty ones—all of humanity—stand before a Judge and books are opened. The record in the books is the basis for the final judgment.
   c. Before the Judge stand all the beautiful, broken, guilty ones, each shut up under sin, every mouth silenced from any defensive appeal or any excuse. The record in the books speaks for itself.

REFLECT FOR A MOMENT

This is Sagan's "bottomless free fall"—mankind "lost in a great darkness." He is right about that, because we're all guilty, and no judge owes a pardon. Atonement must be made. The debt must be paid. Justice must be perfect. That's the bad news.

B. Mercy

1. I once told an audience, "The answer to guilt is not denial. That's relativism. The answer to guilt is forgiveness. And this," I said, "is where Jesus comes in."
2. I have made that point many times to audiences, and every time I say those words, something moves inside me. Forgiveness. Mercy. Repair. Restoration. Rebirth. New life. Hope. This is what each of our souls longs for on the inside.
3. Sagan is right when he says we are lost, but he is wrong when he says there is no one to send out a search party.
   a. Clearly, we can't rescue ourselves. Help must come from outside of Sagan's closed cosmos, from outside of this world.
   b. Here is our message to all the broken souls who know they're broken: The search party has arrived. The Rescuer has come.

c. He is the One who calls to us, "Come to Me, all who are weary and heavy-laden, and I will give you rest. . . . For I am gentle and humble in heart, and you will find rest for your souls" (Matt. 11:28–29).

REFLECT FOR A MOMENT

In his *Confessions*, Augustine of Hippo famously described the proper place of repose for the restless human soul. He wrote, "You have made us for yourself, O Lord, and our hearts are restless until they can find rest in you."

VI. OUR RESTLESS SOULS

A. The restlessness of the human soul, our sense of longing, our yearning to be filled—or maybe yearning to be fixed—is a universal human affliction.

1. It's a malady, though, that has nothing to do with our natural appetites.
2. Satisfying our passions never satisfies the deep hunger of our hearts.

B. Two facts of the human condition lie at the heart of our inescapable sense of longing.

1. One is that we are broken.
2. Two is that it hasn't always been this way.
    a. There remains a remnant of former beauty the brokenness can't destroy, yet something has gone missing that must be replaced.
    b. We feel a "sweet pain . . . a primal memory deep in our souls reminding us of the way the world started—good, wonderful, whole, complete."[39]
    c. We were made for something better, and we scrap and we scrape to climb back up, to return to the heights.

REFLECT FOR A MOMENT

The struggle to affirm our human significance is central to just about every film we have ever seen and every story we have ever read. The "triumph of the human spirit," they say—which is, of course, God's image forcing its way to the surface, to the outside. The exceptions are those dark, nihilistic yarns, the dystopian tales that tell the lie that we are nothing. But note the conflicting visions: the vision buried deep in our humanity, and the contrary vision flowing from the atheistic, nothing-ism view of reality.

INTERACTIVE STUDY

As a group, think of some movies you have seen that showcase the glory, the nobility, and even the tragedy of being human. How does the film make sense of this unique quality of humanity? Explain how the specifics of the movie are examples of the Inside Out dynamic. In what way might the details of the storyline be leveraged in a conversation with a non-Christian to show how well Christianity explains the truths expressed there, while non-Christian views cannot?

C. Atheism cannot explain this.

1. Atheism denies the guilt. It has to. Without Good, there is no Bad.
2. Atheism also denies the beauty and wonder of being human. Again, it has to.
    a. If there's no God, there's no guided design, only biological accidents, physical parts stuck together without reason or purpose—cosmic junk.
    b. Man is nothing and his life means nothing.
3. Atheism has no answer to human brokenness.
4. Atheism leaves us, once again, with nothing.
    a. It can't provide the consolation of true forgiveness.
    b. Our true longing is a hunger that a godless universe simply cannot satisfy, a thirst that humanism cannot quench.
    c. We are fallen. We are guilty. We are lost. And we cry out.

D. Christianity, by contrast, gives us an answer.

1. C. S. Lewis wrote, "If I find in myself a desire which no experience in this world can satisfy, the most probable explanation is that I was made for another world."[40]
2. The Christian worldview makes sense of the actual world we live in.
   a. It makes sense of beauty and meaning and hope.
   b. It also makes sense of the world's brokenness.
   c. The world the Bible describes is the one we hunger for.
3. Notice how vigorously the truths that are already built into us by God assert themselves. That's the inside coming out.
   a. It's a world where transcendent beauty makes sense.
   b. It's a world where longing and hunger can be satisfied.
   c. It's a world where rising up from the fall is possible—a world where there is hope.
4. Here is our remedy, stated simply in a Christmas card I received from a friend: "The birth of Christ . . . invites us to believe that the cries of a broken world have actually been heard—a Savior was born."[41]

AMBASSADOR SKILLS

There are times when good arguments evade you. That's when—maybe—a simple declaration of the truth might be all that's needed. "Come to Me, all who are weary and heavy laden . . ." That's an offer of meat to hunger and drink to thirst.

Take advantage of the Inside Out insight. Touch the existential nerve—that deep, profound desire that throbs in every single fallen human being made in the image of God. Listen carefully in your conversations. Listen for when a person's mannishness speaks. When they tell the truth—and they have to eventually—point it out.

Even though a person can run from God, he cannot run from himself. And that is the key to the Inside Out tactic.

VII. WHAT MAIN POINTS DID WE COVER IN THIS SESSION?

A. First, we learned the basics of the Inside Out tactic.

1. The Inside Out tactic is an insight into what it means to be human that helps us navigate in conversations.
2. Since all humans are made in God's image, then "man is different from non-man," in Francis Schaeffer's words—what he called the "mannishness of man."
3. God has built certain information inside every human being that eventually reveals itself on the outside in a person's words, actions, or attitudes, in ways contrary to their expressed view of the world.
4. Those truths include the awareness that humans have profound value and worth, that we were designed for a valuable purpose, that we are beautiful yet broken and guilty, and our restless souls hunger for rescue.
5. We looked at some examples of how a person's mannishness betrays his false worldview.

B. Next, we learned ways to employ the Inside Out tactic.

1. First, listen to the way people talk.
   a. Listen for when—from their own mouths—their knowledge of reality intrudes on their false philosophies.
   b. Listen for when their words betray their true convictions about the world, even when they don't realize it.
2. Second, exploit that tension by asking questions.

C. Finally, we learned that sometimes an appeal to a person's existential need—their deep human longing—can be more powerful than an argument.

D. In our next session I'll teach you a handful of maneuvers I call "Mini-Tactics" that will be a great addition to your tactical toolbox.

INTERACTIVE STUDY

Self-Assessment

Try to answer the following questions without using your notes.

1. Briefly describe the Inside Out tactic.
   - The Inside Out tactic is not so much a specific maneuver as a ____________, an understanding of what it means to be ____________.
   - Since all humans are made __________, then "man is different from ___________," in Francis Schaeffer's words. He called this the "______________."
   - God's truth that is already on the ________ of every person will eventually real itself on the _______ in their _________, _________, or _________, even though it _________ their own worldview.

2. List three or four things all humans know in virtue of their mannishness.
   - ______________________
   - ______________________
   - ______________________
   - ______________________

3. List three steps to applying the Inside Out tactic.
   - First, __________ to the way people __________, for when their implicit claims about reality __________ their false worldviews.
   - Second, exploit that tension by ____________________.
   - Third, appeal to a person's existential need—their ____________________.

Self-Assessment with Answers

1. Briefly describe the Inside Out tactic.
   - The Inside Out tactic is not so much a specific maneuver as a *frame of mind*, an understanding of what it means to be *a human*.

- Since all humans are made *in God's image*, then "man is different from *non-man*," in Francis Schaeffer's words. He called this the "*mannishness of man.*"
- God's truth that is already on the *inside* of every person will eventually real itself on the *outside* in their *words*, *actions*, or *attitudes*, even though it *contradicts* their own worldview.

2. List three or four things all humans know in virtue of their mannishness.
    - *We have innate value and worth.*
    - *We've been created for a purpose.*
    - *We're broken and guilty.*
    - *Our souls are restless, hungering for rescue.*

3. List three steps to applying the Inside Out tactic.
    - First, *listen* to the way people *talk*, for when their implicit claims about reality *contradict* their false worldviews.
    - Second, exploit that tension by *asking questions.*
    - Third, appeal to a person's existential need—their *deep human longing.*

GOING DEEPER: Information for Self-Study

1. This week, pay close attention to the way people talk, to the implicit messages conveyed about what they think it means to be human. Be alert for expressions of both error and truth conflicting with each other, even though they're coming from the same source.
2. Tell some of your friends about the Inside Out tactic and the insights about being human that lie behind it.
3. Review the foregoing self-assessment exercise so you'll be able to answer all the questions without the prompts.

FOOD FOR THOUGHT

French philosopher Guillaume Bignon found his naturalistic atheism being challenged as he encountered Christ in the New Testament.[42] Nevertheless, the cross confused him. "Why did Jesus have to die?" he asked over and over again as he worked through the historical accounts of Jesus' life. It made no sense to him.

Then something unexpected happened. "God reactivated my conscience," he told me. "That was not a pleasant experience. I was physically crippled by guilt, not knowing what to do about it."

Suddenly it dawned on him. "*That's* why Jesus had to die. Because of *me*. Because of *my* guilt." He immediately surrendered all his brokenness to the only one who could repair it, giving all his guilt to the only one who could forgive. When he did, "the feelings of guilt just evaporated."

SESSION 8

Mini-Tactics

INTERACTIVE STUDY

Demonstrating Mastery

Try recalling the answers to the following questions without using your notes. The answers are located at the end of session 7.

1. Briefly describe the Inside Out tactic.
   - The Inside Out tactic is not so much a specific maneuver as a ______________, an understanding of what it means to be ___________.
   - Since all humans are made _________________, then "man is different from _________________," in Francis Schaeffer's words. He called this the "_________________."
   - God's truth that is already on the ________ of every person will eventually real itself on the ______ in their _________, __________, or __________, even though it _________ their own worldview.

2. List three or four things all humans know in virtue of their mannishness.
   - ______________________
   - ______________________
   - ______________________
   - ______________________

3. List three steps to applying the Inside Out tactic.
   - First, __________ to the way people __________, for when their implicit claims about reality __________ their false worldviews.
   - Second, exploit that tension by ____________________.
   - Third, appeal to a person's existential need—their ____________________.

INTERACTIVE STUDY

Find someone with whom to share your experience from last session's assignment. Did you notice any particular ways that the truth on the inside of a person began to show itself on the outside, even when it contradicted his own worldview? Discuss it together.

I. REVIEW

A. In the last session, we covered the following:

1. We learned a tactic called "Inside Out."
   a. Since all humans are made in God's image, then "man is different from non-man," in Francis Schaeffer's words—what he called the "mannishness of man."
   b. We learned that God has built certain information inside everyone that eventually reveals itself on the outside in that person's words, actions, or attitudes, in ways contrary to their view of the world.
   c. Those truths include the awareness that humans have profound value and worth, that we were designed for a valuable purpose, that we are beautiful yet broken and guilty, and our souls are restless, hungering for rescue.
2. Next, we learned three ways to employ the Inside Out tactic.
   a. First, listen to the way people talk. Listen for when—from their own mouths—their knowledge of reality intrudes on their false philosophies,

betraying their true convictions about the world, even when they don't realize it.

b. Second, exploit that tension by asking questions.

c. Finally, remember that sometimes an appeal to a person's existential need—their deep human longing—can be more powerful than arguments.

B. In this session, we'll cover Mini-Tactics.

1. Mini-Tactics are a handful of modest maneuvers I think will help you in your conversations with others.
2. I call them Mini-Tactics because the concepts are relatively uncomplicated and can be put into play easily when needed.

II. WHAT A FRIEND WE HAVE IN JESUS

A. This tactic trades on the high regard people have for Jesus as an authority, even if they're not one of his followers.

1. There is a tendency for people who are not Christians to make theological points based on what Jesus either said or, presumably, did not say. Jesus has credibility even with those who are not his followers.
2. The person making the appeal is trying to bolster his view by conveniently enlisting Jesus as an ally.
3. It's a smart move, and we can make use of it too.

B. Here is the general principle: pit the challenger against Jesus—not you—whenever you can.

1. Get Jesus on your side and let him do the arguing for you.
2. When your challenger disagrees with you, then, they'll be disagreeing with Christ.

REFLECT A MOMENT

This was my approach when I faced off with New Age guru Deepak Chopra for a national TV debate. Deepak is one of the few people in the world who can be immediately recognized by his first name. I knew it would be a mistake to position my credibility against Chopra's fame. There was someone else on my side, though, who had a lot more firepower than I did: Jesus. If I could position the debate as Chopra versus Jesus ("Dr. Chopra says this, but Jesus says that"), I knew I would fare much better in the eyes of the viewers.

C. Example: Jesus the only way

1. When someone presses you on the "narrowness of Christianity," say, "Well, I understand how you feel, but this was Jesus' view, not mine, and he repeated it often."
2. "Do you think Jesus was mistaken?"

REFLECT A MOMENT

Once I got a letter from a dad whose daughter was competing in a statewide beauty pageant. She was sure to face a question about same-sex marriage—an obvious attempt to marginalize anyone who didn't toe the politically correct line on that issue. He wanted my opinion on the safest way to answer the question, "What do you think about same-sex marriage?" and still be faithful to Christ. Jesus said we should be innocent but shrewd, so I worked out this response I think satisfies both requirements:

> Since I am a follower of Christ, my view on marriage is the same as Jesus' view, one he made clear in Matthew 19. I'll sum it up this way: Jesus' view was that marriage involved *one man, with one woman, becoming one flesh, for one lifetime*. So on the definition of marriage, I stand with Jesus.

You get the point. Disagree with the Christian on this, and you disagree with Christ. That's why this approach should be your first line of response when answering this particular question.

III. STICKS AND STONES

A. Sticks and Stones is a defensive Mini-Tactic meant to blunt the rhetorical force of distractive name calling.

1. Negative labels succeed at marginalizing you because of their ambiguity.
2. Plus, the person using them has changed the subject—from the issue at hand to a question of your character, which is irrelevant to the discussion. This fallacy is called an *ad hominem*.

AMBASSADOR SKILLS

My mom used to say, "Sticks and stones may break your bones, but names will never hurt you." It's a clever saying that encourages us to brush off foolish people, ignore their empty insults, and move on. That's usually good advice. It's not entirely accurate, though. When it comes to thinking carefully, name calling can be a distraction, and so it can do damage. This is where the Sticks and Stones tactic comes in. It's a maneuver to protect you from a certain type of bad thinking and bad manners.

B. Here's how the tactic works:

1. Whenever anyone tries to deflect your point by labeling you with a nasty name—bigot, homophobe, Islamophobe, racist, whatever—always ask for a definition.

2. The impact of these words is often so powerful, you'll have a hard time overcoming them unless you flush out their meanings into the open.

C. There are two advantages of asking for a definition.

1. First, it stops the momentum of the unfair attack, puts the ball in the other person's court, and puts you back in the driver's seat.
2. Second, it forces the other person to think about what he just did.
   a. I suspect most people don't realize they've made a false move when they revert to personal smears. They've been so thoroughly socialized to do this, they don't realize that it's both irrelevant to an issue and also unkind.
   b. Once the challenger spells out what he means, ask him why he thinks it's helpful attacking your character instead of showing where your idea went wrong. Remember, ridicule is not an argument.
   c. Your questions could help take some of the edge off the attack.
3. Name calling is an act of hostility, though, so be sure to be gracious and calm when you ask for a definition and offer your follow-up questions.

IV. MOVING TOWARD THE OBJECTION

A. This tactic is based on the idea that sometimes it's better to move toward an objection and embrace the charge rather than move away from it.

1. I was introduced to this maneuver in a movie. In the opening scenes of *Clear and Present Danger*, a man with connections to the president is found dead in what appears to be a drug deal gone bad. To contain the PR damage, the president's advisors suggest he immediately downplay the relationship and distance himself from the problem.
2. Analyst Jack Ryan suggests just the opposite. "If they ask if you were friends," he counsels, "say, 'No, he was a *good* friend.' If they ask if he was a good friend, say, 'We were *lifelong* friends.' It would give them no place to go. Nothing to report. No story."

AMBASSADOR SKILLS

Sometimes it's tactically smart to run toward a challenge and defuse it. Don't evade; invade. Embrace it. Undermine its relevance. Take the wind out of its sails. In certain situations, that's good advice.

B. Examples

1. Challenge: Imperfect design
   a. In a radio debate with atheist Michael Shermer, I fully expected him to fire off the atheist's standard response to evidence for intelligent design: "If you argue for ID, then you're going to have to deal with the problem of imperfect design."
   b. The problem is, if God designed living organisms, their design would have to be perfect. But there seem to be design flaws. Therefore there was no divine designer.
   c. If that point came up, I planned to follow Ryan's advice and embrace the challenge, moving toward the objection.
      1) "Michael, you're absolutely right. If I'm going to argue for an intelligent designer, then I *am* going to have to deal with that problem. But you're not going to get off that easily."
      2) "One apparent anomaly doesn't nullify the overwhelming evidence for design. That would be like saying a wristwatch wasn't designed because it ran three minutes slow. You're straining a gnat but swallowing a camel."
   d. By moving toward the challenge, I'd blunt the objection by telegraphing to the radio audience I was aware of the difficulty and wasn't shaken by it. Shermer would have "no place to go. Nothing to report. No story."

REFLECT A MOMENT

I know of Christians who are stumped when atheists charge, "There are lots of gods you don't believe in too, such as Zeus, Jupiter, and Thor. We atheists just believe in one less God than you." It turns out, the atheist is exactly right on this point, but it does him no good. Believing in one less God than a monotheist is exactly what distinguishes atheists from Christians, after all. Nothing meaningful follows from this observation. The Christian could simply say, "Yes, you're right. You do believe in one less God than I do. That's what makes you an atheist and me a Christian. We all already know that. So what's your point?" and then watch the challenge fizzle.

2. Challenge: The church is filled with hypocrites.
   a. MTO: Right! Actually, the church is filled with worse than hypocrites—liars, swindlers, fornicators, adulterers, drunks, self-centered egotists, sinners of all sorts.
   b. That's precisely why they need Jesus.
3. Challenge: There's so much evil and suffering in the world. How can there be a God?
   a. MTO: Of course there's so much evil in the world. That's exactly what you'd expect if the Christian account is true. Evil is central to our story.
   b. The Bible doesn't just explain it. It predicts it. We live in a world humans broke, and a broken world produces broken people and broken situations.
4. Challenge: Jesus is a crutch; God is a crutch.
   a. MTO: You're right. Handicapped people need crutches, though. We need God to help us, to hold us up, to forgive us.
   b. We all have crutches. The real question is, "Can your crutch hold you?" What crutch are you leaning on?

AMBASSADOR SKILLS

The next time someone raises an issue or a problem, instead of backpedaling, think for a moment if there might be a way to move toward the objection, embrace it, and defuse it.

C. Summary:

1. Moving toward the Objection is a tactic that's useful when it's to your advantage to agree with a charge rather than oppose it. Sometimes it's possible to cast a negative as a positive, or at least as something inconsequential.
2. Tell them they're right, then show them it doesn't work in their favor the way they think it does. Embracing the complaint when you can defuses it, taking the wind out of the critic's sails.

V. WATCH YOUR LANGUAGE

A. This Min-Tactic is a simple communication tip that will make you more effective as an ambassador for Christ.

1. Much of our Christian lingo sounds like religious noise to outsiders.
   a. Terms like "faith," "belief," "the Bible," "receive Jesus," even "sin"—as important as it is to talk about that—fall on deaf ears.
   b. People have heard this kind of talk before, and they tune out what to them is religious "blah, blah, blah."
2. Worse, Christian lingo can be misleading.
   a. This is especially true of the word "faith," which suggests a kind of useful fantasy, a leap of religious wishful thinking with no reason or evidence.
   b. Nothing like this is in view, of course, with the original biblical concept. Still, it's the way many people (including Christians) mistakenly understand it.

B. To solve the lingo problem, make a habit of finding (and using) substitute words—synonyms—for religious terminology. It will brighten your conversation and improve your communication.

For example:

1. Don't quote "the Bible" or "the Word of God" (both easily dismissed).
   a. Instead cite "Jesus of Nazareth" or "the people Jesus personally trained to follow after him" (the apostles) or "the ancient Hebrew prophets."
   b. When referring to the Gospels, try citing the "ancient biographical evidence" for Jesus, or "the primary source historical documents" for the life of Jesus of Nazareth. That's the way historians see them.
   c. These substitute phrases mean the same thing but have a completely different feel to them. It's much easier to dismiss a religious book than the words of a respected religious figure.
2. I frequently use the phrase "Jesus of Nazareth" instead of "Jesus Christ" or even the more religious-sounding "Christ." My phrase communicates a feet-on-the-ground, real person of history. Plus, those words are fresher to contemporary ears.
3. I also advise that you banish the word "faith" from your vocabulary.
   a. Instead substitute "trust" for the *exercise* of faith ("I have placed my trust in Jesus"), which is the precise meaning of the original biblical term anyway.
   b. Substitute "convictions" for the *content* of faith ("These are my Christian convictions"—that is, "This is what I've become convinced of").
   c. For the same reason, don't talk about your "beliefs." It's too easy to misunderstand that word as a reference to *mere* beliefs, subjective true-for-me preferences. Rather say, "This is what I think is true," or, "These are my spiritual [not 'religious'] convictions."
4. I've even been avoiding the word "sin" lately, not out of timidity but because the English word doesn't seem to deliver anymore.
   a. Instead I talk about our "moral crimes" against God, or our "acts of rebellion," or our "sedition against our Sovereign."

   b. By contrast, please eliminate terms like "blown it" and "messed up" as synonyms for sin. They simply do not capture the gravity of our offense. Rather they end up trivializing our wickedness before God.

5. The word "forgiveness" still seems to have emotional power, but sometimes substitute words like "pardon," "clemency," and "mercy" can put a fresh face on it.

C. Remember, there's nothing wrong with using replacement words.

1. Biblical translation is always a matter of choosing appropriate synonyms for original Greek or Hebrew terms.
2. The goal here isn't to soften the original meaning. Rather the goal is to substitute more vivid, powerful, and precise words for stale, religious language—adding more punch to our point.

AMBASSADOR SKILLS

Watch Your Language is a general guideline reminding you to banish Christian lingo from your vocabulary. That lingo means nothing to non-Christians, plus it can sound annoying, and it can also be misleading. To fix the problem, use appropriate synonyms for stale religious terms. Try to find down-to-earth ways of communicating your convictions to others so they don't tune you out.

VI. THE POWER OF "SO?"

A. The tactic

1. The Power of "So?" employs a simple question ("So?") that disputes the relevance of challenges that sound compelling at first but turn out to be irrelevant to any case against God or Christianity.

2. Whenever someone faults an idea by attacking something about the person who holds it and not by addressing the idea itself, agree with the point for the sake of argument, then ask, "So?"

B. Why the tactic works

1. Many challenges offered by skeptics amount to little more than intellectual trash talk.
   a. These are clever-sounding complaints that have rhetorical impact and may intimidate you, but they have nothing to do with any reasonable case against God or Christianity.
   b. Here is where a bit of reflective thinking coupled with a simple Mini-Tactic can be golden.
2. I want you to see the tactical power of a humble two-letter word.
   a. This word is a little giant, putting the ball back into a skeptic's court and putting you in the driver's seat of an otherwise difficult situation.
   b. When used properly, it can stop a challenger in his tracks, turn the tables, and get him thinking.
   c. That little word, used as a question, is the word "So?"
3. Use this tactic when it's clear to you that the charge fired at your convictions doesn't hit any meaningful target.
   a. Even if we agreed with the claim, nothing useful follows from it.
   b. Your response is to sympathize with the challenge and then simply say, "So?"

C. Examples

1. It's not uncommon to hear a dismissive "Christians are stupid" from a critic.
   a. My response: "You're right. Some of them are. So?"
   b. There are plenty of dull, simpleminded, gullible religious people. So what? Lots of nonreligious people are dull, simpleminded, and gullible too.
   c. Can Christianity be true if some Christians are dumb? Sure. Can atheism be false even if an atheist is brilliant? Of course. The observation, even if true, takes us nowhere. It's just trash talk.

2. Here's another: "Christians are hypocrites."
    a. My response: "Yep, some are. I admit it. So?"
    b. Sure, some religious people don't live up to their convictions. Churchgoers have all sorts of vices.
    c. Therefore what? That Christianity is false? That doesn't follow. The shortcomings of Christians tell us nothing about the merits of Christ.
3. Here's a popular one: "You're a Christian because you were raised in America. If you were raised in Iraq, you'd be a Muslim."
    a. My answer: "Probably. So?"
    b. Even if that's true, what does it tell us about the merits of Christianity versus Islam? Nothing. What does it tell us about the merits of theism versus atheism? Nothing.
    c. This may be an interesting observation about culture, or psychology, or anthropology, but it tells us nothing about the truth or error of any specific religious claim.
    d. By the way, if the atheist were raised in Iraq, he wouldn't be an atheist. Clearly, this is not a legitimate argument against atheism, so the same approach can get no traction against Christianity.

AMBASSADOR SKILLS

Whenever someone faults an idea by attacking something about the person who holds it and not by addressing the idea itself, you know they're being irrational. Here's why: you cannot refute a view by attacking something else. The question for the atheist is simple: "Does God exist?" He'll never get anywhere close to an answer to that question by focusing on human anthropology, human psychology, or human culture. Each of those is irrelevant to the question. These attempts are nothing more than genetic fallacies or psychogenic fallacies or ad hominems—all irrational missteps, not thoughtful responses. Anyone advancing such an appeal is being unreasonable.

D. Summary of the Tactic

1. So listen carefully to a challenge, then consider what the consequences are for your view *even if the observation is accurate*. If there's nothing that you're aware of, point it out using this tactic. Then see what happens.
2. Rhetorical tricks like these may be daunting to the untutored who can't see through them, but they don't work. Weed out the trash talk using the Power of "So?" Mini-Tactic, and you'll have a lot less nonsense to deal with.

VII. WHAT MAIN POINTS DID WE COVER IN THIS SESSION?

A. In this session we learned five relatively uncomplicated Mini-Tactic maneuvers that will help you in your conversations with others.

B. The Mini-Tactics

1. What a Friend We Have in Jesus
   a. This tactic is based on the fact that Jesus has credibility even with those who are not his followers.
   b. The person making the appeal is trying to bolster his view by conveniently enlisting Jesus as an ally.
   c. You can use the same approach. The general maneuver is to pit the challenger against Jesus—not against you—whenever you can.
2. Sticks and Stones
   a. This is a defensive tactic meant to blunt the rhetorical force of distractive name calling.
   b. Whenever anyone tries to deflect your point by labeling you with a nasty name—bigot, homophobe, Islamophobe, racist, whatever—always ask for a definition.
      1) First, your question stops the momentum of the unfair attack, puts the ball in the other person's court, and puts you back in the driver's seat.

2) Second, it forces the other person to think about what he just did—changed the subject by attacking your character instead of addressing the issue at hand.

3. Moving toward the Objection
   a. Sometimes it's better to move toward an objection and embrace the charge rather than move away from it.
   b. Don't evade; invade. Undermine its relevance. Take the wind out of its sails. See if you can find a way to cast a negative as a positive, or at least show that the objection is inconsequential.
   c. Tell them they're right, then show them it doesn't work in their favor the way they think it does.
4. Watch Your Language
   a. Christian lingo sounds like religious noise to outsiders. Plus, it can be misleading.
   b. Correct this problem by making it a habit to find (and use) substitute words—synonyms—for religious terminology. It will brighten your conversation and improve your communication.
   c. The goal isn't to soften the original meaning. Rather the goal is to substitute more vivid, powerful, and precise words for stale, religious language—adding more punch to our point.
5. The Power of "So?"
   a. This Mini-Tactic employs a simple question ("So?") to dispute the relevance of challenges that sound compelling at first but turn out to be irrelevant to any case against God or Christianity.
   b. Carefully consider the challenge, then reflect on the consequences it has for your view *even if the observation is accurate.*
   c. If there's nothing that you're aware of, point it out. When someone faults an idea by attacking something other than the idea itself, sympathize with the challenge, then simply say, "So?"

INTERACTIVE STUDY

Self-Assessment

Try to answer the following questions without using your notes.

1. Briefly describe the What a Friend We Have in Jesus Mini-Tactic.
   - This tactic trades on the idea that Jesus has __________ even with those who are __________________.
   - The general maneuver is to __________________ against _______ whenever you can.
   - When your challenger disagrees with _____, then, they'll be disagreeing with __________________.

2. Briefly describe the Sticks and Stones Mini-Tactic.
   - This Mini-Tactic is meant to blunt the rhetorical force of distractive __________________.
   - When people call you a name instead of addressing the issue itself, they have cleverly ________________________________.
   - This fallacy is called an __________________.
   - Whenever anyone tries to deflect your point by calling you a nasty name, always ________________________________.
   - Next, ask the person why he thinks it's helpful attacking your ______ instead of showing where your ____________________. Ridicule is not an __________________.

3. Briefly describe the Moving toward the Objection Mini-Tactic.
   - Sometimes it's better to move _______________ an objection rather than move ______________ from it.
   - See if you can cast a __________ as a ____________, or at least as something ________________.

- If so, tell them they're ________, but show them it doesn't ____________________ the way they think it does.

4. Briefly describe the Watch Your Language Mini-Tactic.
   - Christian lingo sounds like ____________________ to outsiders, plus it can be __________________.
   - Make a habit of using accurate ____________________ for religious terminology.
   - Try to find down-to-earth ways of __________________ your __________ to others so they don't ____________________.

5. Briefly describe the Power of "So?" Mini-Tactic.
   - Many challenges turn out to be ____________________ to any case against God or Christianity.
   - Consider what the consequences are for your view even if the ________________________.
   - When this happens, __________________ with the challenge and then simply say, ____________

SELF-ASSESSMENT WITH ANSWERS

1. Briefly describe the What a Friend We Have in Jesus Mini-Tactic.
   - This tactic trades on the idea that Jesus has *credibility* even with those who are *not his followers*.
   - The general maneuver is to *pit the challenger* against *Jesus* whenever you can.
   - When your challenger disagrees with *you*, then, they'll be disagreeing with *Christ*.

2. Briefly describe the Sticks and Stones Mini-Tactic.
   - This Mini-Tactic is meant to blunt the rhetorical force of distractive *name calling*.
   - When people call you a name instead of addressing the issue itself, they have cleverly *changed the subject*.

- This fallacy is called an *ad hominem.*
- Whenever anyone tries to deflect your point by calling you a nasty name, always *ask for a definition.*
- Next, ask the person why he thinks it's helpful attacking your *character* instead of showing where your *idea went wrong.* Ridicule is not an *argument.*

3. Briefly describe the Moving toward the Objection Mini-Tactic.
   - Sometimes it's better to move *toward* an objection rather than move *away* from it.
   - See if you can cast a *negative* as a *positive*, or at least as something *inconsequential.*
   - If so, tell them they're *right*, but show them it doesn't *work in their favor* the way they think it does.

4. Briefly describe the Watch Your Language Mini-Tactic.
   - Christian lingo sounds like *religious noise* to outsiders, plus it can be *misleading.*
   - Make a habit of using accurate *substitute words or synonyms* for religious terminology.
   - Try to find down-to-earth ways of *communicating* your *convictions* to others so they don't *tune you out.*

5. Briefly describe the Power of "So?" Mini-Tactic.
   - Many challenges turn out to be *irrelevant* to any case against God or Christianity.
   - Consider what the consequences are for your view even if the *observation is accurate.*
   - When this happens, *sympathize* with the challenge and then simply say, *"So?"*

VIII. FINAL REFLECTIONS

> The more you sweat in training, the less you bleed in battle.
>
> —Marine Corps training adage

A. First, know your Bible well enough to give an accurate answer for the faith that is in you. "Do your best to present yourself to God as one approved, a worker who does not need to be ashamed and who correctly handles the word of truth" (2 Tim. 2:15 NIV).

B. Second, study these tactics.
   1. Become familiar with how they work.
   2. Know when to use them and how to initiate them.
   3. Teach them to others when you can. It's a great way to solidify these concepts in your own mind.
   4. Use the tactics. They can be a powerful game changer for you, but *if you don't do it, it doesn't work.*

C. Third, push yourself beyond your comfort zone.
   1. Be courageous. Begin to mix it up with others before you feel adequately prepared. Trust me on this; it's good advice.
      a. You'll learn best by immediately using the information you have gained.
      b. You'll take a few hits along the way, but you'll also give a few back in a good way.
   2. You'll also learn what the other side has to offer, which often isn't very much.

D. Fourth, don't be discouraged by outward appearances.
   1. Don't get caught in the trap of trying to assess the effectiveness of your conversation by its immediate, visible results.
   2. Even though a person pushes back at what you say, you may have still put a stone in his shoe.
   3. The Holy Spirit can use even your modest efforts to bring others to the truth.
   4. Remember, before any harvest there always has to be a season of gardening. These things often take time.

E. Finally, live out the virtues of a good ambassador (see the "Ambassador's Creed" at the end of this session).

1. Represent Christ in a winsome and attractive way.
2. You—God's own ambassador—are the key to making a difference for the kingdom.
3. With God's help, show others that Christianity is worth thinking about.

INTERACTIVE STUDY

Think—Pair—Share

Reflect together on specific things you found especially helpful in this study guide. How have you been encouraged by this material? How do you plan to use it in the future?

FOOD FOR THOUGHT

A Stone in His Shoe

In some circles, there is pressure for Christian ambassadors to close the sale as soon as possible. When pressed for time, they say you should get right to the meat of the message. Get to the gospel. If the person doesn't respond, at least you've done your part, right? Shake the dust off your feet and move on.

A wise ambassador, though, weighs his opportunities and adopts an appropriate strategy for each occasion. Sometimes the simple truth of the cross is all that's needed. The fruit is ripe for harvesting. Bump it and it falls into your basket.

Usually, though, the fruit is not ripe; the nonbeliever is simply not ready. He may not have even begun to think about Christianity. Dropping a message on him that, from his point of view, is meaningless or simply unbelievable probably won't accomplish much. It might make things harder. He may reject a message he doesn't understand and then be harder to reach next time around.

Here is my own more modest goal: I want to put a stone in his shoe. All I want to do is give him something worth thinking about. I want him to hobble away on a nugget of truth he can't easily ignore because it continues to poke at him.

Whether the opportunity is a short one with a transient audience or a long one with a close friend, my goal is the same—place a stone in his shoe.

Some people are good closers. They're good at leading people across the threshold and into the kingdom. What they don't realize is that harvesting often comes easily for them because, in God's sovereignty, many ambassadors came before them to plant the seed, water the soil, and pull the weeds, one by one tending to the plant and cultivating healthy growth until the fruit was ripe and ready to reap.

Follow the strategy I use when God opens a door of opportunity. I don't know how long the door will be open, so I pray quickly for wisdom (Col. 4:5), and then I ask myself, "In this circumstance, what is one thing I can say, one question I can ask, one thought I can leave that will get him thinking?"

Then I simply try to put a stone in his shoe.

Ambassador's Creed

An ambassador is:

- *Ready.* An ambassador is alert for chances to represent Christ and will not back away from a challenge or an opportunity.
- *Patient.* An ambassador won't quarrel but will listen in order to understand, then with gentleness seek to respectfully correct those in opposition.
- *Reasonable.* An ambassador has informed convictions (not just feelings), gives reasons, asks questions, aggressively seeks answers, and will not be stumped by the same challenge twice.
- *Tactical.* An ambassador adapts to each unique person and situation, maneuvering with wisdom to challenge bad thinking, presenting the truth in an understandable and compelling way.
- *Clear.* An ambassador is careful with language and will not rely on Christian lingo or gain unfair advantage with empty rhetoric.
- *Fair.* An ambassador is sympathetic and understanding toward the opposition and will acknowledge the merits of contrary views.

- *Honest.* An ambassador is careful with the facts and will not misrepresent his opponent, overstate his own case, or understate the demands of the gospel.
- *Humble.* An ambassador is provisional in his claims, knowing that his understanding of truth is fallible, and will not press a point beyond what his evidence allows.
- *Attractive.* An ambassador will act with grace, kindness, and good manners and will not dishonor Christ in his conduct.
- *Dependent.* An ambassador knows that effectiveness requires joining his best efforts with God's power.

Notes

1. Note Paul's comments on spiritual warfare in Ephesians 6:10–20.
2. Sometimes defensive and offensive apologetics are called "negative" and "positive" apologetics, respectively.
3. Here I'm referring to either a denial of metaphysical realism (a denial that there is a mind-independent world that can be known) or a denial of epistemological realism (if there is a "real world," it can't be known). Postmodernists affirm a certain kind of "truth," but it is not truth as we normally understand it (a belief is true if it matches the way the world actually is—truth as correspondence to reality).
4. Hugh Hewitt, *In, But Not Of: A Guide to Christian Ambition* (Nashville: Thomas Nelson, 2003), 166.
5. If you follow STR's radio program, either live or via podcast (available at str.org or iTunes), you will notice that I take pains not to abuse callers who disagree with me.
6. The best way to see how this is done is to observe it in action. This can be done through the STR weekly radio podcast—a talk show where I engage callers of all persuasions on a large variety of issues. My intent in this program is to give my callers something to think about ("put a stone in their shoe") as I challenge their views on spiritual or moral concerns and advance the Christian worldview as an alternative. During these encounters, I am constantly alert for tactical opportunities.
7. I'm grateful to Kevin Bywater of Summit Ministries for improvements he helped make on the questions used in Columbo.
8. Hewitt, 167.
9. Ibid., 172–73.
10. Find more detail on this argument at str.org. Search under the key word "evil."
11. That is, there are no squares that are not squares because it is a logical impossibility. All laws of logic are self-evidently true and need no defense. In fact, any argument against the validity of the basic laws of logic must employ those laws to deny them.
12. That which is known before, "prior to," a process of discovery, in particular, discovery by sense experience. The word is often used to describe philosophical commitments that are brought to the table as defining elements of a debate before other relevant evidence is considered. These commitments determine how the evidence will be viewed or whether it will be considered at all. "*A priori*" is contrasted to "*a posteriori*," that which is known after looking to experience, specifically sense experience.
13. "This is an 'apples and oranges' error because it mixes up two ideas that don't belong together, [e.g.,] 'What does blue taste like?'" Norman L. Geisler and Ronald M. Brooks, *Come, Let Us Reason Together: An Introduction to Logical Thinking* (Grand Rapids: Baker, 1990), 108.
14. Sometimes the issue of Jesus being the only way of salvation is best answered by Jesus Himself and the men He trained to carry His message after Him. Order a copy of the STR booklet *Jesus: The Only Way—100 Verses* at str.org to find a hundred different references—nine different lines of argument—in the New Testament demonstrating the necessity of faith in Christ for salvation.

15. A number of STR resources develop this idea, including the CD *Evil, Suffering, and the Goodness of God*. Or you can go to str.org and do a search on the word "evil" to find multiple entries. See especially the article titled "God, Evolution, and Morality."
16. Jonathan Wells, *Icons of Evolution, Science or Myth?* (Washington, DC: Regnery, 2000), 79–80.
17. J. P. Moreland, *Scaling the Secular City: A Defense of Christianity* (Grand Rapids: Baker, 1987), 92.
18. Note: Stand to Reason has a valuable booklet titled *Jesus, the Only Way: 100 Verses* to enable you to biblically answer the charge that "all roads lead to Rome." It is an affordable resource that every Christian should have. Order a copy at www.str.org.
19. This view is called "scientism." Empiricism, the claim "I only believe what I can perceive with my senses," self-destructs in the same way. The truth of the proposition itself cannot be perceived with the senses.
20. C. S. Lewis, *Mere Christianity* (New York: Macmillan, 1952), 31.
21. For the full transcript, see "A Conversation with Lee" at www.str.org. It is a delightful lesson in the use of the Suicide tactic.
22. The article "Theistic Evolution: Drifting Toward Darwin," at str.org, develops this idea more thoroughly.
23. C. S. Lewis, *God in the Dock* (Grand Rapids: Eerdmans, 1970), 272.
24. Francis Schaeffer, *The God Who Is There*, in *The Complete Works of Francis Schaeffer*, vol. 1 (Wheaton, IL: Crossway, 1982), 140–41.
25. In any given situation, there may be a number of ways to express the truth that follows from your *reductio*.
26. See Romans 13:3–4.
27. Christina Hoff Sommers, "Teaching the Virtues," reprinted in *AFA Journal*, January 1992, 15.
28. Schaeffer, 142.
29. Students of the STR course, "Making Abortion Unthinkable—The Art of Pro-Life Persuasion," will recognize "Trotting Out the Toddler" as an important tactic in refuting prochoice arguments. The course is available at str.org.
30. Note: This was the very approach I took with the witch from Wisconsin in session 1.
31. On occasion you will encounter what I call "benevolent steamrollers," overly excitable, but not hostile.
32. Richard Dawkins, *River out of Eden* (New York: Basic, 1996), 133.
33. Richard Dawkins, *The God Delusion* (Boston: Houghton Mifflin, 2006), 31.
34. Note, I'm not suggesting that Dawkins's specific complaint is sound, but rather that objectivist moral assessments like this are completely at home in the actual world, not in his faux reality.
35. Francis Schaeffer, *He Is There and He Is Not Silent*, in *The Complete Works of Francis Schaeffer*, vol. 1 (Wheaton, IL: Crossway, 1982), 278.
36. Bill Nye's June 5, 2010, Humanist of the Year Award acceptance speech in San Jose, California.
37. Carl Sagan, *Pale Blue Dot: A Vision of the Human Future in Space* (New York: Random House, 1994), 6, 51.
38. Ibid.
39. Gregory Koukl, *The Story of Reality* (Grand Rapids: Zondervan, 2017), 83.
40. C. S. Lewis, *Mere Christianity* (New York: Simon and Schuster, 1952), 106.
41. My thanks to Jonathan Noyes.
42. Guillaume Bignon, "How a French Atheist becomes a Theologian: Inside My Own Revolution," *Christianity Today* (November 17, 2014), *www.christianitytoday.com/ct/2014/november/how-french-atheist-becomes-theologian.html.*